This Book Belongs To

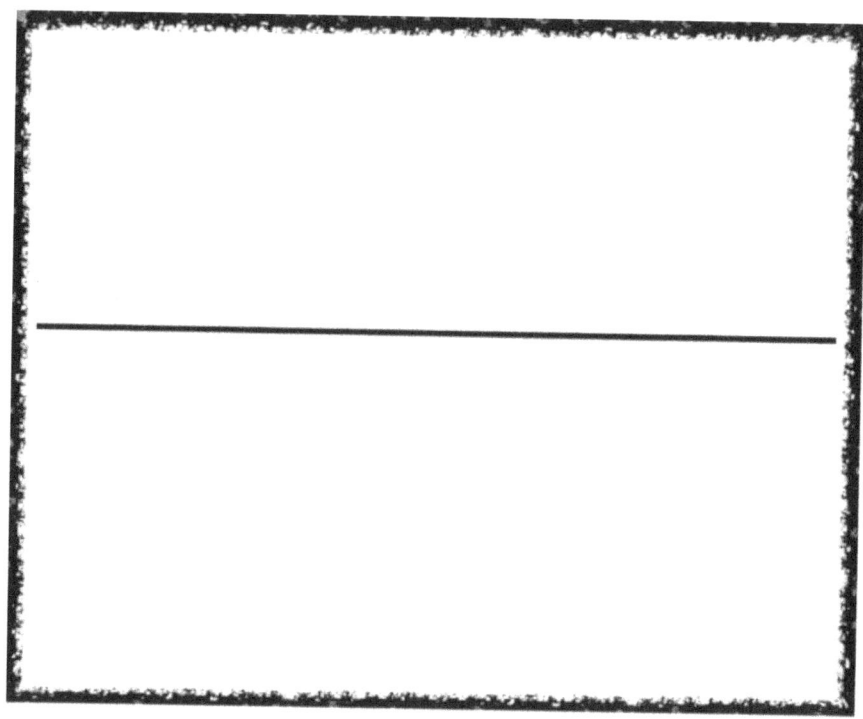

Find Us On

Website www.adropfromeden.com

Instagram https://www.instagram.com/adropfromeden/

Twitter https://twitter.com/adropfromeden

Facebook aromatherapy group https://www.facebook.com/groups/adropfromeden

Facebook Ministry Group https://www.facebook.com/groups/adropfromedenministry

This book is dedicated to my brother CG

whom without his wisdom and

encouragement wouldn't have been

possible.

About The Author

Hello, God's children my name is Felicia Patterson, I hold a degree in psychology, aromatherapy as well as am an Ordained Minister. Journaling has helped me through some very tough times in my life along with my faith and I thought why not combine the two. I could go on about my accomplishments but instead, I would like to share with you a personal story of what the power of faith and prayer can do.

About The Author

I was born with a rare spinal condition. My parents reached out to all the greats, but all said there was no treatment and just keep me comfortable until my time came. After months of searching and praying, a young and brilliant neurosurgeon came up with a plan that would hopefully work. Prior to what was to be a series of surgeries, I wanted to see the Happy Hunters that were a few hours away from us. Things were tight but my parents made it happen but only had fifty dollars to travel on. We got to the motel got cleaned up and walked across the street where they were giving the sermon. At this time, I had lost all function of my lower extremities and I had to be carried into the church. Prior to the sermon, they were passing the plate. We only had enough to get back home, so we don't have anything to spare. As they were passing the plate my mom put the fifty dollars in. The lady minister whom I will never forget asked my dad to sit me beside her. While her husband was giving the sermon, she was rubbing my back. My parents had communicated with them through email, but she had no knowledge of who we were or my condition. After a while, she asked my mom and another woman to take my hands and walk me around the church. I had not walked in months yet practically ran around the church. After it was over, we were headed for the lobby when the same woman that walked with me around the church came up to my mom and said, "God told me to give you this" and gave her two twenties and a ten. Our Life is a testament that through all the challenges, loss, and despair that we must hold to our faith and trust that we are all here for a purpose.

About Your Journal

Bible

Coloring Page

Reflect

What's on my heart

My Prayers

THE NEXT FEW PAGES WILL EXPLAIN HOW TO USE YOUR
JOURNAL

BIBLE STORIES

Each week 52 total features a new bible story to reflect your thoughts on throughout the week giving you time to understand the meaning behind story

COLORING

Each week features a coloring page based on that weeks bible story. Coloring works other areas of the brain, allowing the brain a chance to relax, and the space needed to shift gears. In turn, it allows the brain time to focus on the topic at hand.

R EFLECT

Each week contains a "Reflect" page with questions and thoughts inspired by that weeks bible story.

W hats on my heart & my prayers

What's on my heart is a place to write the personal things going on in your life what week and what you may needs Gods guidance in.

My Prayers is a place you can list your weekly prayers and see how God answers your prayers throughout the year.

Table Of Contents

Table Of Contents

THE FIRST DAYS

In the beginning,

God made Heaven and Earth. The earth was empty and had no form. Everything was dark, so God said, "Let there be light," and there was light. God saw that the light was good. So, he divided the light from the dark. He called the light "day" and the dark "night." This is how the first day began.

On the second day, God said, "Let there be a great space, and I will call it sky,". As a result, God created the sky and the clouds. God was happy, and this was the end of the second day.

On the Third Day. This was when God created the deserts, mountains, and islands. God took water and shaped them into oceans, lakes, ponds, and rivers "so that dry land may appear." The dry land was named "Earth" and water the seas, but the earth was still baron. So, God created plants and trees of wide varieties. Then God was happy with today's work.

On the fourth day, God said, "let there be lights in the sky to separate the day from night. He called the bigger light the "sun" and the smaller light the "moon". He then added twinkling stars that could only be seen at night. These lights will not only be used to tell night from day but to separate the days, seasons, and years. Evening came, and God was happy.

On the fifth day, God said, "Let the water be filled with living things. Furthermore, let birds fly in the clouds above the earth." He filled the oceans, rivers, ponds, and lakes with colorful fish and sea life. He then raised his hand to the sky and filled it with beautifully colored birds. God then blessed them all, saying, "have many young and grow in number. Evening came, and God was happy with today's work.

On the sixth day, God thought, "This is right and good," So God created human beings in his image. He created them male and female God blessed them and said, Be fruitful and multiply.

On the seventh day, God looked over all He had created and smiled. Happy with the world around him. God blessed the seventh day and made it a holy day. He then rested from all his work in creating the world.

Moral God is the creator of everything we see.

REFLECT

Why is it important to know how
God felt about what He created?

WHAT'S ON MY HEART

_____

_____

_____

_____

_____

_____

_____

_____

_____

_____

MY PRAYERS

_____

_____

_____

_____

_____

_____

_____

_____

_____

_____

_____

_____

THE GARDEN OF EDEN

God created Adam from the dust of the earth and gave him life by breathing into his nostrils. God made a beautiful garden for Adam to live in. The Garden was called Eden and was full of many beautiful things. The Garden was full of many trees, flowers, birds, and animals.

God had made man in His image to keep Him company and look after the earth. God gave Adam the honor of naming all the animals in the Garden. Soon Adam became lonely. So, God put Adam into a deep sleep and created a woman from a rib on Adam's side. When Adam awakened that morning, he discovered his wife, Eve, sleeping next to him. Eve awoke as Adam took her hand. Adam was delighted.

God told Adam and Eve that caring for the Garden was their job. God blessed them And said, "This is all for you. Help yourself to anything, but, I warn you, don't eat from the tree in the middle of the Garden. That tree gives knowledge of good and evil. It is a forbidden fruit.

One day, when Adam and Eve were in the Garden, the serpent, the wittiest of all the animals, convinced Eve to eat the forbidden fruit from the tree. Eve shared the fruit with her husband. Adam and Eve ate the prohibited fruit from the tree, even though they were told not to. This was the first sin. As a result, God was forced to expel them from the Garden. They would have to pay for their sins. They would have to work very hard to get food from the ground. They would feel pain and die at the end of a very hard life.

Moral

Never disobey God's commands, as they exist to protect you from sin.

REFLECT

What do you think caused Adam
and Eve to disobey?

WHAT'S ON MY HEART

_____

_____
_____
_____
_____
_____
_____
_____
_____
_____

MY PRAYERS

_____

_____
_____
_____
_____
_____
_____
_____
_____
_____

CAIN AND ABLE

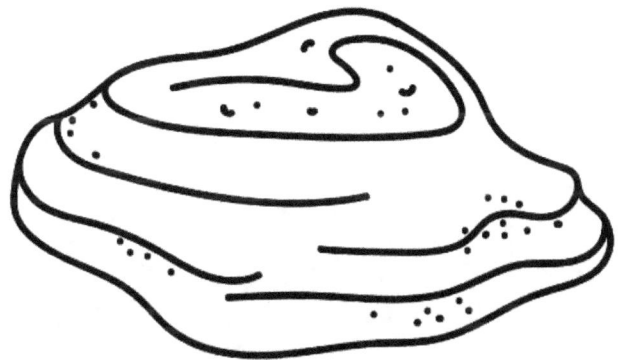

After Adam and Eve were banished from the garden, their life required hard work just like God said it would. Things would never be the same because of their sinful choices. They still reflected gods image, but that image was now tarnished.

Adam and Eve had two sons, Cain and Able. Their firstborn son Cain became a farmer, while Able was a shepherd. Both sons brought a sacrifice to the Lord. Cain brought some of his harvests. He said, "I've got some good crop, but many pieces are bruised. God won't mind if I keep some good pieces for myself".

Meanwhile, Able brought the firstborn of his animals and the best of his meat as an offering. God saw the heart behind each offering and liked Abel's sacrifice. Cain was angry. He didn't want God to determine what he should give. God warned Cain that rage wasn't healthy because it was self-centered and fueled by pride. Cain was envious of Abel and angry with God. The Lord cautioned Cain that his self-centered rage was deadly.

Cain, on the other hand, did not heed God's warning. He remained angry. Cain sought to conceal his sin and Abel's death as soon as possible. One day in the field with Abel, Cain let his jealousy get to the best of him and killed his brother.

While Cain pretended not to know where Abel was, God was already aware of Cain's involvement in Abel's death. God knows everything, so sin can't be hidden from God.

God was saddened when He observed Cain's sin because He knew the price of sin. God had to punish Cain for his sin, so He exiled him from His presence. Cain was upset that he had to abandon God.

Moral

Sin leads to sadness and separation from God

REFLECT

Why do you think Abel's offering was seen differently by God than Cain's?

WHAT'S ON MY HEART

_____

MY PRAYERS

_____

NOAHS ARK

"Get married and start a family," God told man and woman. That's what they did, and the Earth was filled with people. However, many people did terrible things, and the Earth became a weed-infested garden. As a result, God chose to flood the Earth.

Noah, a righteous and honest man, received a message from God. Make a wooden ark for yourself. Find two of each animal species, gather their food, then load them onto the ark." The fact that Noah relied on God led him to do what the Lord had told him. Then God said something to Noah. "Create a safe place for yourself and your family on the ark, for it will rain for 40 days and 40 nights." Although there will be a big flood, the ark will keep you safe.

" Rain flooded the Earth for 40 days and 40 nights, just as God had said, and all living creatures were wiped away. Noah's family and animals, on the other hand, were safe within the ark.

The ark was left high on a hill after the flood. A breathtaking rainbow was seen in the sky above, and it was the very first one ever formed. The rainbow was God's promise that such a flood would never happen again. And God instructed Noah and the animals to begin remaking the world.

Moral

Noah had to be patient and believe in God's plan for him. Noah's family made it to safety. God promised Noah that he would never flood the Earth again. The rainbow symbolizes these promises. Rather than worrying about what other people think, we must remain faithful to God.

REFLECT

Why was God angry with humans?

WHAT'S ON MY HEART

_____

_____
_____
_____
_____
_____
_____
_____
_____
_____

MY PRAYERS

_____

_____
_____
_____
_____
_____
_____
_____
_____
_____
_____

THE RAINBOW OF GOD'S PROMISE

The flood had come to an end. Every living thing on the planet was killed.

Only the animals and people on the ark survived. Noah understood what he needed to do first. He erected an altar in the name of God and presented him with gifts.

Noah expressed his gratitude to God for sparing the lives of his family. "God promised to "never flood the earth again."

The passage of time will eternally be marked by the passage of the four seasons. God told Noah; the world is yours. "Do it right." The first rainbow appeared out of nowhere in the sky.

Now, whenever a rainbow appears, people think back to the promise God made to Noah.

Moral

We must trust in God and always hold to our word.

REFLECT

Why did God send a rainbow?

_____

_____

_____

_____

_____

_____

_____

_____

_____

_____

_____

_____

_____

_____

_____

_____

_____

_____

WHAT'S ON MY HEART

_____

_____

_____

_____

_____

_____

_____

_____

_____

_____

MY PRAYERS

_____

_____

_____

_____

_____

_____

_____

_____

_____

THE TOWER OF BABEL

In this story, you'll learn how God deals with pride. It all started with Nimrod, a king.

Everything was going well. Every single person in the world spoke the same language. Some of the people eventually made their homes in a place known as Babylonia.

Then King Nimrod decided to become famous. He wanted everyone to know who he was and what a fantastic person he was. He persuaded the people of Babylonia that if they built a tower that reached heaven, they could also be great.

As a result, the people began manufacturing bricks for the Tower of Babel. It was hard work, but the people wanted everyone to know that they had built the tower that reached the heavens, making their work even more complicated.

The people were also convinced that by building the tower, they would remain united as one. Their pride soon took over, and all they could think about was becoming famous worldwide for making the world's giant and best tower.

God, the all-knowing, was aware of what was happening and decided to visit the people and see the tower they were building. God could tell from the attitude of the people's hearts that they were more concerned with themselves and the tower than with him. He was disappointed and angry with them.

God responded, "People seem to believe they can accomplish anything since they all speak the same language. They've already started to turn away from me, and there won't be anything good left for them soon; all they'll do is sin. I will make it, so no one speaks the same language, so they don't understand each other, making it impossible for them to sin.

People could no longer understand each other after God said this. People began speaking in various languages, including French, Spanish, Chinese, and many other languages. It appeared as though they were babbling and making multiple strange noises.

This was the start of all languages. Consider what would have happened if the people had not attempted to build the tower in the first place and instead concentrated on God. Perhaps today, we would all speak the same language.

REFLECT

Why was it necessary that God scatter mankind out across the earth?

_____

_____

_____

_____

_____

_____

_____

_____

_____

_____

_____

_____

_____

_____

_____

_____

_____

_____

WHAT'S ON MY HEART

MY PRAYERS

ABRAHAM'S COVENANT

There was once a faithful man dedicated to his vocation and blessed by God. Unfortunately, the one thing he is missing is a child of his own. The Lord promised Abram that He would be the father of many countries, and Abram was thrilled and eagerly anticipated the arrival of his promised son. That did not happen for a long time, though. His wife Sarai didn't give him a son.

Sarai tried to get Abram to marry her maidservant, Hagar from Egypt, to do things her way. As a result of Abram's actions, Hagar became pregnant with a son. When the child was born, he was called Ishmael.

One day, Abram received a visit from three men, all of whom were treated with utmost respect and courtesy. These men were God and his angels who were dressed up. They told Abram that Sarai would have a son by the same time next year. Sarai giggled because she thought she was too old to have a child. This was not the promised child because the Lord had pledged to Sarai a son and that through him, He would bless Abram. The Lord also gave Abram and Sarai new names, and from then on, they were known as Abraham and Sarah because Sarah means "Princess," and she would become the mother of many countries.

God kept his promise. Sarai had a son at the same time the following year. When they told Sarah that she would have a son, she laughed. They named him Isaac, which means "laughter." This is because when they told her she was with a child, she laughed.

Moral

God is faithful, and He always keeps His promises.

REFLECT

How does doubt affect **your** everyday life?

Why is it important to trust God everyday?

_____
_____
_____
_____
_____
_____
_____
_____
_____
_____
_____
_____
_____
_____
_____
_____
_____
_____
_____

WHAT'S ON MY HEART

_____

_____

_____

_____

_____

_____

_____

_____

_____

_____

MY PRAYERS

_____

_____

_____

_____

_____

_____

_____

_____

_____

_____

_____

SODOM AND GOMORRAH

Sodom and Gomorrah were twin cities that were so tangled in sin that they would not listen when the people talked about God. One day Abraham saw three men approaching. He could tell they weren't regular men by their appearance, one of whom looked to be the Lord God Himself in human form. The Lord told Abraham he would destroy the cities because of the people's sins.

Abraham, being known as the Father of Many Nations, wanted to save the people. Abraham said. "Perhaps there are still some good people who are there." Would you save the cities if 50 good people lived there?" The Lord said, "If I discover fifty good people in Sodom, then I will spare the city for their sake." Abraham concluded. Would you still destroy the cities if there were forty-five good people? "If I can locate forty-five good people, I won't destroy the cities." This conversation continued until Abraham asked if there were only five good people would he save the city? God told Abraham, "I will save the cities if I find five good men." Abraham remained silent since he didn't need to say anything else. The Lord then proceeded toward Sodom as a man, and Abraham turned returned to his tent.

Abraham asked Lot, his brother, years earlier to choose a place to live. Lot chose Sodom, although it was a sinful city. Lot was hoping to bring the people closer to God. The angels visited the town looking for people that would be saved. They decided to visit Lot, who was the only good man in the city. Recognizing they were angels, Lot welcomed them into his home and cooked them a meal.

When people in Sodom learned that outsiders were visiting Lot, they rushed to his door and attempted to kidnap the angels so they could punish them. Lot was terrified to see this, but the Angels encouraged him to calm down. All those sinful men were blinded instantly by the two angels, and they stumbled around in the dark. The angels asked Lot if he had any more family. They informed Lot to gather his family and get out of the city as soon as possible because it was going to be destroyed due to all the sins. Lot gathered his wife, daughters, and possessions and was ready to leave the city. Lot was warned to hurry, flee the city, and don't look back, or you will die. "Hurry, and get out of town since the Lord will destroy it," Lot and his family headed up the mountain when his wife decided to look back and turned into a pillar of salt. Lot and his daughters obeyed God's orders and escaped unharmed.

Moral

Always do your best not to defy God. The only thing that comes from sin is punishment and death. Lot was a good man and obeyed God to the best of his abilities. Lot's wife failed to follow God's order not to look back. She did and was punished for her actions.

REFLECT

What is sin? Is it a word, thought, or our actions?

_____
_____
_____
_____
_____
_____
_____
_____
_____
_____
_____
_____
_____
_____
_____
_____
_____
_____

WHAT'S ON MY HEART

MY PRAYERS

ISAAC AND ABRAHAM

As a result of the destruction of Sodom and Gomorrah, Abraham relocated to a region known as Gerar, not far from the Great Sea. After many years of waiting, Sarah gave birth to the son God had promised her and Abraham. When Sarah gave birth to Isaac, Abraham was a hundred years old. They gave this little boy the name Isaac, as God said she would.

Abraham and Sarah were delighted to have a child, and their excitement prompted them to organize a large feast for all the people to celebrate their son Isaac. Every time they wanted to worship, they would build a stone altar and sacrifice animals on it as an offering to God. they usually chose a sheep, a goat, or any animal utilized for nourishment.

This giving was known as a sacrifice. Many people then worshipped idols and did many strange and horrible things. They believed that offering their god the most valuable living things they owned as a sacrifice would please them. This cruel belief drove them to sacrifice their children on their altars as offerings to the Gods. God wanted to show Abraham, all his descendants, and those who were expected to follow him that he was not happy with how the horrible people killed others as offerings. At the same time, God wanted to see how faithful and obedient Abraham would be to his commands, how much Abraham trusted God, and how great Abraham's faith in God was. Then, God came up with a unique way to test Abraham. "I want your son Isaac, whom you love and cherish, to go to Moriah's land. I'll show you a mountain, and you must present Isaac as a sacrificial offering. Abraham never questioned or defied God, so he did as God asked.

He knew that Isaac was the child God had promised. God had said that Isaac would have children and that Isaac was a great man. He couldn't understand how God would not keep his promise to Isaac; if Isaac was sacrificed as an offering, the rest of what he was told was a lie. But Abraham did as God asked. He traveled northward toward the mountain with two young men and a donkey packed with wood for the fire while his son Isaac walked behind him. They traveled for two days and slept in the open country beneath the stars.

On the third day, Abraham saw the mountain far ahead. As they approached the mountain, Abraham said to the young men, "Sit here while I go up with my son Isaac to pray on the mountain; I will be back soon." Abraham hoped that God would somehow bring Isaac back to life. He grabbed the wood from the donkey, gave it to Isaac, and the two of them headed up the mountain. After a while, Isaac asked Abraham,
"Dad, where is the lamb we're supposed to sacrifice to God?"

Abraham was taken by surprise he replied, "My son, you don't have to be concerned; God Himself will provide the lamb we'll use." Soon they arrived at the top of the mountain. Abraham constructed a stone altar, bound Isaac's hands and feet, and placed him on the altar. Abraham then lifted his hand, holding a knife ready to sacrifice his son.

Just as Abraham was about to kill him, an angel spoke to Abraham! Abraham!

-

"Lord, here I am," Abraham responded, "speak for I can hear you." The angel told Abraham, "Do not sacrifice your son. There is no need to harm him. For now, I know you love God more than anything and are loyal to him. He was delighted to learn that sacrificing his son was not God's will. When Abraham turned around, he noticed a ram entangled in the bushes. Abraham took the ram and presented it as an offering in place of his son. And when Abraham predicted that God would provide a steed, his prayers were answered.

Abraham named the location where he constructed the altar Jehovah-Jireh, which means "The Lord will provide" in Abraham's language. The extraordinary sacrifice has resulted in a great deal of good. It revealed to Abraham, as well as to Isaac that Isaac belonged to God. God did not want children or men to be sacrificed as offerings, and while all the people around them gave these sacrifices, the Israelites did not, offering oxen, sheep, and goats as sacrifices. " It also anticipated a day when God would send his Son, Jesus Christ, to die for the world like Abraham had offered his son as a sacrifice. All of this was taught during a church service on Mount Moriah. Abraham resided in Beersheba for many years, where he later made his home. After the offering on the mountain, he and his family returned to Beersheba. After so many years, Sarah, Abraham's wife, and Isaac's mother, died at the age of 122. The people gave Abraham a cave called Machpelah near Hebron. He used it to bury his wife, Sarah.

Moral

God hates it when people are being killed. Therefore, he warned us not to kill. Anyone who murders is wicked and will be punished by God.

REFLECT

Why do you think Abraham was able to trust that God had a plan?

WHAT'S ON MY HEART

_____
_____
_____
_____
_____
_____
_____
_____
_____
_____

MY PRAYERS

_____
_____
_____
_____
_____
_____
_____
_____
_____
_____
_____

THE COAT OF MANY COLORS

This is the story of a young man named Joseph. They lived in Canaan, where his grandfather was originally from, where his father Jacob was.

Joseph was seventeen years old. He had ten older brothers and one younger brother. Imagine having eleven brothers. Joseph's father spent more time with him because he was one of the youngest sons and became very dear to him. As a result, Jacob had Joseph's robe custom-made. (Jackets were not standard at the time. Therefore this was a unique jacket.) It was stunning and contained every color you could imagine. When Joseph's older brothers saw this, they were jealous. Joseph's brothers were envious of him because they thought his father favored him and because he received the unique coat. They were so jealous that they couldn't even say anything kind to him.

One day, Joseph had a dream and went to tell his brothers. He said, "Guess what? I had an unusual dream last night. We were out in the field putting up grain bunches when my bunch rose to its feet while yours gathered around and bowed to me." Joseph continued while his brothers exchanged disgusted looks. In another dream, the sun, moon, and eleven stars all bowed to me, and I woke up. "Do you have any idea who you are?" According to the brothers. "Do you believe you are superior to the rest of us? Do you believe we'll ever bow down to you?" This just added to the brothers' hatred for Joseph. "Those are unusual dreams," his father replied.

A few days later, Joseph's father asked him to check on his brothers. They were out in the fields working. As a result, Joseph set out to find them. When the brothers noticed Joseph in the distance, they devised a plan to kill him. Upon hearing this, Joseph's elder brother Reuben suggested that they not kill him but dump him in a well out in the field. "Let's not kill him." He said this because he would return after the other brothers had left and rescue Joseph. When Joseph arrived, they ripped off his gorgeous coat and tossed him into the well.

A little while later, a group of people approached, claiming to be interested in selling some items in Egypt. "Why don't we sell him to these guys," one of the brothers suggested. "That way, we won't have to see him again, and we won't have to kill him." The other brothers thought this was a good idea, so they sold him to people traveling to Egypt.

Reuben was working at the time, so he didn't see what had happened. When he returned to the well, he discovered Joseph had vanished. He had been sold to a powerful man named Potiphar, an Egyptian Pharaoh's assistant.

The remaining brothers grabbed Joseph's magnificent coat and soaked it in animal blood before returning it to their father. When the father saw this, he screamed, "Some animal has killed my son!" Even though Joseph began his life as an enslaved person, the Lord was with him and helped him.

As a result, Potiphar appointed him as his helper and entrusted him with responsibility for everything. The difficulty arose when Potiphar's wife lied to her husband about Joseph, prompting Potiphar to have Joseph imprisoned. The Lord was still with Joseph, and the warden's son assigned him the responsibility of overseeing all of the inmates. He never had to be concerned since the Lord was with him.

After Joseph had been imprisoned for a while, Pharaoh had a cupbearer and baker sent to him. Each of them had a dream one night. They told Joseph about their dreams, and he told the cupbearer that he would be released shortly. "Please inform Pharaoh of my situation and request that he get me out of here," Joseph pleaded. When the cupbearer was released, he completely forgot what Joseph had done. As a result, Joseph spent another two years in prison. Until the Pharaoh had a strange dream that no one could explain. Joseph was taken to Pharaoh after the cupbearer remembered what Joseph had done for him. "Are you able to interpret dreams?" Pharaoh questioned. "I can't do it, but God will help me," Joseph answered. Pharaoh told Joseph about his dream, and Joseph replied, "God is warning you. There will be seven years during which nothing will grow, and there will be no food for everyone."

"How can I help?" Pharaoh questioned. "You've been shown what to do by God. There will be seven perfect years before the bad ones. The food will be so plentiful that there will be enough for everyone. So you should save a little bit of each year's harvest. You will have enough to get through the bad years." "Joseph stated." Pharaoh trusted all Joseph said and appointed him as the ruler of Egypt. People traveled from all around the world to buy grain from Joseph because they were hungry. Joseph's brothers were among those present. Joseph recognized his brothers when they arrived, but they had no idea who he was. (They hadn't seen him in more than ten years.) Because he was a significant leader, the brothers all bowed to him.

After several meetings with his brothers, Joseph could no longer contain himself and told his brothers, "My name is Joseph! Is my dad still alive?" His brothers, on the other hand, were afraid to respond. After that, Joseph stated, "Please come in. I'm the one you sold, your brother! Because God has sent me here to save people from starvation, you need not be concerned or angry with yourselves for selling me." So his father, siblings, and families joined Joseph in Egypt, where they had all the food they needed.

Moral
A simple story about **love, redemption, and forgiveness.**

REFLECT

What Did Joseph's Coat of Many Colors Symbolize?

_____
_____
_____
_____
_____
_____
_____
_____
_____
_____
_____
_____
_____
_____
_____
_____
_____
_____
_____
_____

WHAT'S ON MY HEART

_____

_____

_____

_____

_____

_____

_____

_____

_____

_____

MY PRAYERS

_____

_____

_____

_____

_____

_____

_____

_____

_____

MOSES IN THE BASKET

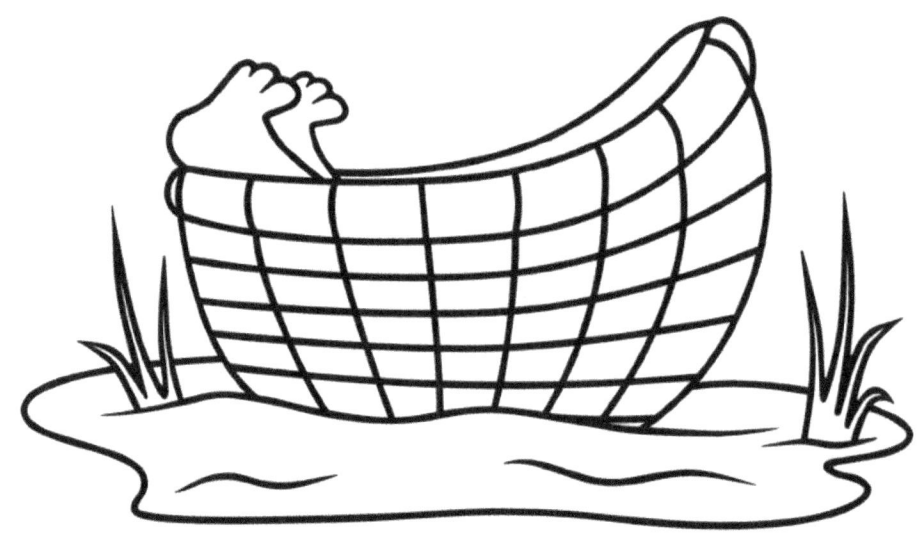

Years have passed since Noah's family began their journey around the world. Many Egyptian kings, known as Pharaohs, came and went during those years. One Pharaoh despised the Israelites, the people who came from the sacred land of Israel. As a result, he enslaved them. However, one Israelite mother loved her child and did not want him to grow up a slave. Baby Moses was hidden in a basket designed to float down the Nile River.

The infant was placed in a basket and sent down the river by his mother. Miriam, the baby's older sister, hid in the bushes and watched the basket floating down the river. Picking up the basket, the Pharaoh's daughter discovered the infant. "It's a boy!" the Pharaoh's daughter said with delight. "I'm going to keep him and give him the name Moses. But who will look after him?" Miriam approached the daughter of the Pharaoh and stated, "I know an Israelite woman who can be the baby's nurse." The nurse entrusted in helping care for Moses was none other than his biological mother.

Moral

God's presence as Savior was evident in Moses' early life. Moses' parents saved him from death by hiding him in a basket on the Nile. The basket symbolizes the ark, which carries Noah and his family to safety.

REFLECT

Moses' mother was brave in sending her child, encased in a basket, into the unknown waters of the Nile. Who found and claimed the baby?

WHAT'S ON MY HEART

_____

_____
_____
_____
_____
_____
_____
_____
_____

MY PRAYERS

_____

_____
_____
_____
_____
_____
_____
_____
_____
_____

THE PROMISED LAND

Moses was raised in the palace of Pharaohs in Egypt. However, Moses was an Israelite and dissatisfied with the Pharaoh's decision to make the Israelites enslaved people. As a result, Moses left the palace to work as a shepherd. Their lives were complicated even though they worked hard.

God, too, was worried. He didn't want his people to be enslaved in any way. God appeared to Moses in the form of a burning bush one day as he was tending to his livestock. A voice from the bush reached out to Moses.

Moses replied, "I am here." "I am God," declared the voice from the burning bush. Moses was terrified. He'd never had a conversation with God before.

" You must help me," God instructed Moses. I've come to release the Israelites from their Egyptian slavery. I will guide you on what to do, and you will be responsible for leading the Israelites out of Egypt and into the Promised Land.

"However, how can I lead the Israelites?" Moses thought. "I'm just a shepherd," she says. They're not going to follow me." Yes, they will, God replied. I'll show proof that I'm on your side, and they'll come with you."

God said, "Throw down your stick." Moses' wooden stick became a snake when he dropped it! God said, "Pick it up." Moses snatched the serpent and turned it back into a stick. "If you show this to the Israelites, they would believe you. "As a result, Moses returned to Egypt, confident in his ability to guide the Israelites to the Promised Land.

Moral

Sometimes we forget that our blessings come from God. We should always be thankful for the many blessings that God gives us.

REFLECT

Why was Moses not allowed to enter the Promised Land?

WHAT'S ON MY HEART

_____

MY PRAYERS

_____

MOSES AND THE BURNING BRUSH

Moses was one of the best people ever to live.

He was one of the most influential people in history. However, he did not consider himself wise or a great man. He was happy with the work he was doing. However, God had a mission for Moses and prepared him for this task during his years in the desert. At that time, the Israelites still carried heavy loads and enslaved people laboring in Egypt to make bricks and build towns. The king who had treated the people had died, but unfortunately, the one who took over was just as bad. He was known as Pharaoh, as this was the title given to all Egyptian kings.

Moses was feeding his flock on the top of Mount Horeb (Often called Mount Sinai). On the mountain, Moses noticed a bush that appeared to be on fire. He waited for the fire to go out, but it didn't. "I'm going to have a look at this unusual thing," Moses said to himself. "It's a bush on fire, yet it's not burning." - Moses was climbing the mountain when he heard a voice calling his name, "Moses, Moses!" Just as he reached the summit, Moses heard the voice again, calling him by his name. - "Here I am," he responded. - And the voice told him, "Moses, do not come closer, but remove your sandals from your feet, for you are standing on holy ground." - As a result, Moses removed his sandals and approached the flaming bush. "I am the king of kings, the God of your father, Abraham, Isaac, and Jacob," said a voice from the burning bush. I have seen the injustices and evil that my people have endured in Egypt, and I have heard their cries as I am their Lord. I will come to deliver them from the hands of the Egyptians and bring them back to their homeland, Canaan, a good and prosperous land. Now come, for I will send you to Pharaoh, king of Egypt, to bring my people out of Egypt." -

Moses saw that getting the Israelites out of Egypt and away from their king's authority would be a monumental task. He was terrified to embark on such a huge responsibility, so he turned to the Lord and said, "Oh God, I am a shepherd here in the forest, and this mission is far too great for me to do." It seems complicated to me to go to Pharaoh and carry your people out of Egypt." - "Certainly, I will be with you, and I will assist you in this important mission," God said to Moses. I'll send you a signal that I'm with you. You will bring my people to this mountain after they have been freed from Egypt, and they will worship me here." - "If I go to the children of Israel in Egypt and tell them that the God of their fathers has sent me, they will ask me, Who is this God?" Moses asked God. What is his given name? Because they have endured so much, I am concerned that they have lost sight of their Creator." - You recall that Moses had been out of Egypt and away from his people for forty years, a long time, and he didn't know if they had continued to worship God throughout that time.

"I am I AM THAT I AM," God said to Moses, "the One who lives forever." Go to your people and tell them, I AM THAT I AM sent me to you. Do not be afraid; go to your people and tell them what I have said to you, and they will listen to you and believe; and you will take the leaders of your tribes, the chief men among them, and go to

Pharaoh the King, and tell him, 'Let my people go, that they may worship their God.'

On the other hand, Moses needed a sign to show his people and the Egyptians that God sent him. When he requested God for a sign, God replied, "What is that in your hand?" "It's a rod, my shepherd's staff, which I used to direct the sheep," Moses explained. - "Throw it to the ground," God said. - Then Moses threw it down, and it transformed into a serpent. Moses was terrified. And God told Moses again, "Bring thy hand under thy bosom beneath thy garment," which Moses did, and his hands were transformed, becoming as white as snow and covered in rough skin, like a leper's hand. He glanced at it with dread and panic. "Put your hand in your bosom again," God instructed him. - Moses did so, and when he removed it, his hands were like the other, with pure skin, and no longer looked like a leper's hand. "If they do not believe you when you go to speak my words, give them the first sign, and let your rod become a serpent," God told Moses. If they still don't believe you, offer them the second sign: transform your hand into a leper's hand and recover it as you did before. And if they continue to refuse to believe, take some river water and transform it into blood. Don't be scared; go tell your people and the Egyptians who I am." - But Moses refused to go, not because he was afraid, but because he believed he was unfit for such a huge responsibility. "God, Father," he replied to the Lord, "you know I'm not a strong speaker; I'm slower to speak; how am I right for this task" - "Am I not the Lord, who formed a man's mouth?" God says. I'll be with thy hands and teach thee what to speak if you go." - "O Lord, appoint another man for this task; I cannot do it,"

Moses pleaded. - "You have a brother named Aaron who can speak well; as I speak to you now, he is on his way to see you in the wilderness; speak to him, and he will help you; let him speak and show you the signs that I have given you," God stated. - In the end, Moses listened to the voice of Heaven and followed it. He returned home with his flocks from Mount Sinai to his father-in-law Jethro. He then traveled to Egypt, where he met his brother, who was on his way to see him. The two brothers, Moses and Aaron, then proceeded to the elders of Israel in Goshen's territory. They told the people what God had spoken and followed through on the signs God had given them. "God has heard all our troubles," the people said, "and he will finally come to set us free." - They were overjoyed, and they thanked God for not forgetting them, for God never fails those who call on him.

Moral

Keep praying to God in times of trouble, for He never ignores those who call upon him.

REFLECT

How did God first reveal himself to Moses
and why?

_____
_____
_____
_____
_____
_____
_____
_____
_____
_____
_____
_____
_____
_____
_____
_____
_____
_____
_____
_____
_____

WHAT'S ON MY HEART

_____

_____

_____

_____

_____

_____

_____

_____

_____

MY PRAYERS

_____

_____

_____

_____

_____

_____

_____

_____

_____

_____

MOSES AND PHARAOH

Having delivered the words that God had given Moses and Aaron to the people of Israel, they went to meet Pharaoh, the King of Egypt. (Remember that Pharaoh was the name given to all Egyptian kings.)

When Moses and Aaron first approached Pharaoh, they did not request that the people be allowed to leave Egypt and never return. Instead, they stated: "Our God, the Lord God of Israel, has directed all our men and us to journey three days into the wilderness to worship him there; and God speaks to you through us, saying: Let my men go so that they may serve me."

Pharaoh, on the other hand, was outraged. - he stated, "Moses and Aaron, why are you calling your people away from their jobs? He yelled! Return to your tasks and ignore your people. I understand why the Israelites fear heading into the desert since there aren't enough jobs to keep them busy. I'll assign them more work."

The Israelites were mainly responsible for manufacturing bricks and building walls for Egypt's pharaohs. "Let them make as many bricks as possible, but don't give them any straw," Pharaoh ordered. - Many of the Israelites were enraged at Moses and Aaron for adding to their burdens, - "May the Lord God punish and judge you! You promised to lead us out and free us, but you've only added to our pain!" -

"Take your brother Aaron, go to Pharaoh again, and show him the signs I gave you," God said. - So they went into Pharaoh and pleaded with him to release the people in the name of the Lord. Pharaoh then said, - "What is the name of the Lord? Why should I follow His commands? What proof do you have to provide for me to believe God genuinely sent you?" - When Moses set his rod down, it turned into a snake. However, Egypt's wise men already knew this. They put down their rods, and their rods transformed into snakes as well. But the fact that Moses's rod consumed their snakes was astonishing. And when Moses picked up the serpent, it changed back into a rod in his hand. However, King Pharaoh refused to heed God's command because he was unimpressed by the miracle Moses performed.

Then Moses waved his rod over Egypt's waters, including the Nile River, canals, and lakes. In front of Pharaoh's eyes, he raised his rod to strike the water. And all the water turned to blood, and all the fish in the river died; and a terrible stench rose from the ground, nearly killing the Egyptians. Pharaoh, on the other hand, refused to listen and would not allow the people to worship God.

Moses changed the blood back into the water after seven days but warned Pharaoh that if he did not obey, another plague would strike. Pharaoh, on the other hand, would not just let the Israelites leave the land. Then Moses stretched out his rod, and frogs swarmed the entire land. They spread out like a large army across the fields, filling the houses and the palace. When Pharaoh noticed that the people were trembling, he said, "Pray for me to your God; ask him to take away the frogs, and I'll let them go." - The frogs were then taken away by God when Moses prayed. Despite this, Pharaoh didn't keep his word and refused to let the Israelites leave. Then Moses raised his rod, as God had instructed, and hit the dust, which became infested with lice and fleas. But Pharaoh refused to listen, so God sent vast swarms and clouds of flies throughout the land, filling their homes with them and covering the sky. The most amazing part is that the Israelites did not have all of this tragedy in their homes.

After that, Pharaoh began to cave. "Why do you feel compelled to leave Egypt to worship God? Here in this land, worship him." - Moses, on the other hand, stated, - "We must make an offering when we worship the Lord, and our offerings are animals that the Egyptians worship. The Egyptians would be enraged if we offered a sacrifice of animals they consider as gods." - -"Well," Pharaoh answered, "you may go away, but not too far, and make certain you all return." - Pharaoh broke his promise when Moses and Aaron eliminated the plague. And God dispatched his angels to slaughter all the animals in Egypt, but to spare those that lived in the land of the Israelites. Pharaoh, on the other hand, was persistent. He ignored God's instructions. Then Moses and Aaron took the ashes from the fire and hurled them into the air like a storm. Then, all of a sudden, boils began appearing on persons and animals throughout the country. Despite this, Pharaoh refused to obey.

Then God instructed Moses to extend his rod toward the heavens. And then a terrible storm descended upon the region. And then, a huge black cloud appeared, thunder rumbled, and lightning flashed through the skies as the rain began to fall; harmful particles within the rain killed plants. It destroyed all of the crops in the area, as well as the fruits on the trees. The Egyptians had never seen anything like this before. Pharaoh was scared again and agreed to let the people go, but when God stopped the rain in response to Moses' request, he broke his promise and refused to let the Israelites leave the land again.

After the rain, vast clouds of locusts descended, devouring every plant on their territory. For three days after the locust, there was deep darkness, no sunlight, no moon, and no stars. Pharaoh, on the other hand, will not let the people go. So he told Moses one day, - "Remove yourself from my sight. Please don't let me see your face again. If you enter my presence, you will be killed." - "As you said, I shall no longer see your face," Moses remarked. - And God spoke to Moses, saying, - "There will be one more plague, after which Pharaoh will be willing to release the people. He'll expel you from the country. Prepare your people because their time will soon come.

Moral

Being stubborn as a child or an adult is not of the Lord, and it may bring more problems when you disobey God. Pharaoh was so determined that he didn't care about God's word, which brought issues for him and his people. Failure to obey God brings punishment. Always obey God.

REFLECT

What did Pharaoh do after having the dreams? Why did he react this way?

_____
_____
_____
_____
_____
_____
_____
_____
_____
_____
_____
_____
_____
_____
_____
_____
_____
_____

WHAT'S ON MY HEART

MY PRAYERS

THE PASSOVER

While all these devastating plagues descended upon the people of Egypt, the Israelites in Goshen were safe because they were under the protection of God. The waters haven't turned bloody, and there haven't seen any flies or locusts to harm them. While the rest of Egypt remained dark, the sun shone brightly in Goshen's land. This gave the Egyptians the impression that the Israelites' Gods' people were safe. As a result, the Israelites found themselves suddenly wealthy. They presented the Israelites with gifts of gold and silver, as well as gemstones and other precious items of all kinds, to win their favor and earn God's love. "You are to go out of Egypt in a few days," Moses told the crowd, "so gather together, get your families and your twelve tribes in order, and prepare to march out of Egypt."

- Moses stated, "God must inflict one more plague on the Egyptians before they let you go. Therefore, you must maintain vigilance and strictly adhere to God's instructions, for if you don't, God's final and most terrible plague will descend upon your homes. The Lord's angel will pass through the country at midnight, and every house's eldest child will die. The son of Pharaoh, the sons of every wealthy individual, and the son of every beggar who has no home will perish. But if you follow my instructions to the letter, your family will be free."

So Moses instructed them on what to do. Each family was given the task of locating and sacrificing a lamb. They had to sprinkle some of the lamb's blood at the entrance, on the top of the door, and each side of the building. They were then to prepare and cook the lamb meat to eat. And no one should leave their home that night because the angel of God would be outside, and he could be killed if they met him.

Israel's children followed Moses' instructions. They sacrificed the lamb, sprinkled the blood, and ate the meat for their evening meal as God had instructed. And they named it the Passover Supper because the angel passed over when he saw the doors sprinkled with blood. As a mark of respect for this memorable night, when God spared his people from death, the Israelites were instructed to have this meal on the same night every year. And this is how The Israelites' feast, known as "The Passover," began.

Moral

At the beginning of the Moses story, Moses' mother places him in a basket in defiance of the Egyptians to save him. She had no way of knowing that this one act would lead to the redemption of their people, but Moses returned to lead the Jewish people out of Egypt. This speaks to the core concept that one person can make a difference.

REFLECT

Why did the Jewish people have to go through such hardship before being redeemed?

_____
_____
_____
_____
_____
_____
_____
_____
_____
_____
_____
_____
_____
_____
_____
_____
_____
_____
_____

WHAT'S ON MY HEART

MY PRAYERS

MOSES PARTS THE RED SEA

As God asked, Moses led the Israelites out of Egypt, and the Egyptians chased them. When God appeared in the form of a cloud, Moses recognized it as a signal and proceeded to follow the cloud. He led the Israelites to the edge of the Red Sea.

The Israelites were terrified. The Pharaoh's soldiers were just behind them, and the sea was in front of them. They felt trapped. Was Moses mistaken about God's signs? Moses paused beside the stream, unsure of what he should do. Then Moses reached his hand over the sea, and God split it in half. There was a dry trail. The Israelites proceeded down the route, walking between sea wafer walls. They had crossed the Red Sea and were on the other side. Behind the Israelites, the Egyptians ran along the dry route. "Wave your staff across the sea," God ordered Moses. The sea was blown back into place when Moses raised his staff, covering the Egyptians. The Israelites had been freed!

Moral

If you need the Lord's help, call upon him, and he will help you.

REFLECT

Why did the new king conclude that he must treat the Israelites harshly? What was he trying to prevent?

_____
_____
_____
_____
_____
_____
_____
_____
_____
_____
_____
_____
_____
_____
_____
_____
_____
_____
_____
_____

WHAT'S ON MY HEART

_____
_____
_____
_____
_____
_____
_____
_____
_____

MY PRAYERS

_____
_____
_____
_____
_____
_____
_____
_____
_____
_____

FOOD RAINS FROM HEAVENS

In the aftermath of Marah, Israel arrived at a place with twelve springs. They took a break behind some palm trees. However, they soon found themselves in a scorching, arid desert with little food.

Everyone was complaining to Moses. They wept and said," We should have died in Egypt." "That'd be better than dying in this desert." God also spoke to Moses. He responded, "I'm going to shower heaven for you." "You'll go out every day and gather enough for that day."

The following day, they noticed small white flakes that looked like frost on the ground. They inquired, "What is it?" Moses said, "This is the bread God has given you." "Collect as much as you need." No leftovers should be kept. They'll go bad." They gathered as much as they needed each morning. However, as the sun became too intense, it melted and fell to the ground. Some people attempted to keep it overnight. It was nasty and worm-infested by morning.

This food was called "manna" in Israel, which means "what is it?" They ate manna every day for the following forty years. They never went hungry. When Israel arrived in Canaan, the manna stopped falling.

Moral
The lesson learned from manna is not only that God provides, and not only that God provides in times of crisis, but also that God provides daily and that we are required to go out and seek it once more.

REFLECT

When we are scared, what can you
remember to encourage us?

WHAT'S ON MY HEART

_____
_____
_____
_____
_____
_____
_____
_____
_____
_____
_____

MY PRAYERS

_____
_____
_____
_____
_____
_____
_____
_____
_____
_____
_____
_____

THE 10 COMMANDMENTS

Israel's population traveled for three months. They reached Mount Sinai at last. Straight from the sand, a vast mountain emerges. The location of Moses' encounter with the burning bush lies nearby. Israel set its camp here, in front of the hill. Moses heard God's voice from the mountain. Don't let anyone touch this mountain; It's a sacred location. Soon, they will all witness me ascending to the mountain's peak. All of Israel gathered up the hill to meet God three days later. A cloud of smoke surrounded Sinai. God had rained fire down upon it. The entire mountain shook violently, terrifying the people.

An increasingly loud trumpet started to sound. Moses communicated with God, and God responded to him through the thunder. They believed they would die. They pleaded, "Don't let God speak to us any longer." On the mountain, Moses entered the dense cloud shielded by darkness. To the peak of the mountain, God called him. There, for forty days, he and God spoke. God shared with him the laws that Israel needed to follow. Moses received two stone tablets from God. The Ten Commandments were written by the hand of God himself on these tablets.

Moral

To establish rules and forbid actions such as murder and theft.

The Ten Commandments

1. Thou shalt have no other gods before me.

2. Thou shalt not worship any graven image.

3. Thou shalt not take the name of the Lord thy God in vain.

4. Remember the sabbath day to keep it holy.

5. Honor thy father and the mother.

6. Thou shalt not kill.

7. Thou shalt not commit adultery.

8. Thou shalt not steal.

9. Thou shalt not bear false witness against thy neighbor.

10. Thou shalt not covet thy neighbor's wife.

REFLECT

How is god laws meant to encourage us?

WHAT'S ON MY HEART

_____
_____
_____
_____
_____
_____
_____
_____
_____

MY PRAYERS

_____
_____
_____
_____
_____
_____
_____
_____
_____
_____

THE WALL OF JERICHO

Jericho was a city that was on top of a hill. High, sturdy walls surrounded it. The Israelite soldiers could not scale the walls to seize the town because they were too tall. Joshua, a leader of the Israelites, sought God's assistance.

Joshua was ordered by God, "Your soldiers should march around the city. Seven trumpeters should lead the way. Do this without making a sound for six days and March seven times around Jericho on the seventh day, blowing the trumpets and shouting. The city will be yours.

The soldiers marched silently around the city walls for six days. The people of Jericho mocked and screamed at the Israelites. The troops wanted to yell back daily, but Joshua warned them not to: Shhh!" The army arrived on the seventh day. They marched seven times around the city. The seven men then blasted their trumpets, and the Israelites all yelled. Jericho's walls shook and crumbled. God had promised that the Israelites would take the city.

Moral

Follow God, even if the journey seems impossible or unexpected.

REFLECT

What lessons did God want the children of Israel to learn from they way they conquered Jericho?

_____

_____

_____

_____

_____

_____

_____

_____

_____

_____

_____

_____

_____

_____

_____

_____

_____

WHAT'S ON MY HEART

_____

_____

_____

_____

_____

_____

_____

_____

_____

_____

_____

MY PRAYERS

_____

_____

_____

_____

_____

_____

_____

_____

_____

SAMSON AND DELILAH

There was a time when Israel's people were at war with the Philistines. God assisted the Israelites in defending their land by making one of their men the most muscular man on the face of the earth. This was Samson.

To defeat Samson and win against Israel, the Philistines needed to know the secret of his power. Samson's hair held the key to his incredible strength. "Refrain from cutting your hair; God warned, "If you don't listen, you'll lose your power."

They sent Delilah, a wise lady, to discover Samson's secret. Delilah questioned Samson about his strength. If I'm bound by seven leather straps, I lose my power. Samson was well aware that she intended to deceive him. As a result, he said, "Don't you know?"

Delilah bound Samson down with seven straps while he slept that night. The Philistines attacked in the morning, believing Samson was safely bound. Samson, on the other hand, was unstoppable. "You've made a fool of me," Delilah growled to Samson.

Delilah pressed Samson for his secret repeatedly. And Samson had a habit of tricking her. Samson eventually gave up and told her his secret. "If my hair is cut." I'm going to lose my strength." Delilah cut Samson's hair when he fell asleep.

Samson's strength diminished, and the Philistines kidnapped him. They disabled him and imprisoned him by removing his eyes. On the other hand, the Philistines forgot to cut Samson's hair, and it grew back. To celebrate their triumph, the Philistines carried Samson to a crowded temple. Samson snatched a large pillar from the temple and yanked it down on the Philistines. "Make me strong again so that I may obtain retribution for my eyes!" Samson prayed softly to God.

Moral

To allow God to help us make the right choices.

REFLECT

What lessons can we learn from Samsons life?

_____
_____
_____
_____
_____
_____
_____
_____
_____
_____
_____
_____
_____
_____
_____
_____
_____
_____

WHAT'S ON MY HEART

MY PRAYERS

DAVID AND GOLIATH

The Palestinian army entered the Valley of Ilah one day, intending to attack Israel. King Saul decided that Israel would not launch an initial attack because it would harm them. However, war broke out between the two nations. Israel's population had to deal with Palestine for 40 days. In the army of Palestine, there was a fighter by the name of Goliath. Who resembled a giant. The average warrior was significantly shorter than Goliath. Simultaneously, he would destroy many Israeli soldiers. Because of this, nobody came forward to challenge him. There was no one in King Saul's army to face Goliath, which caused more problems for him and his soldiers.

One day, David's father gave him orders to go to the front lines and report on his siblings. When David arrived at the battleground, he observed that Goliath was loudly challenging everyone.

Goliath said, "Whoever wants to fight me must come before me. If I win, you will be my slave; if I lose, we will all be your slaves." After hearing what Goliath had to say, David decided to take on the giant.

David contacted King Saul to request permission to participate in the battle.

David spoke to the king, "King, I am coming to you from the battleground." After hearing David's remarks, the king asked: "David, have you seen Goliath? I saw that Goliath is giving us a challenge, and I want to accept it. Permit me to fight him." Look at Goliath's body, and then look at your own body. You cannot battle him. He will instantly end you. David, I can't let you fight because you're too young.

Don't worry about who is small or big; David tried to reason again. Just give me the order to take on Goliath. The king then inquired, "Well, how will you fight him, having never engaged in combat?"

David retorted I give up on my God, victory, and defeat. God is the one who safeguards me from the lion and other dangerous animals when I go into the forest with my sheep. God will deliver me from the devil. And will support me as I take on Goliath.

The king permitted David to go to war after hearing him speak and seeing his confidence in God. He told him, "Well, you can fight Goliath, but you must wear armor for your safety before heading to the battlefield. You must follow my commands, or I will not approve. David explained to the king that he did not have the practice of wearing armor and that the weight of it would be too much for him to bear. He declared, "My God is my true savior, and he will keep me safe and give me the courage to fight."

When the king asked David to remove his sling, he said, "This is my weapon, and God has given me the ability to use it. Please don't worry, my king, and allow me to go to war toward the battleground. Along the way, he gathered five stones to use in the slingshot.

I shall successfully finish you with the help of God and his might. When David arrived at the battlefield, he stood before Goliath and said, "Look down here, Goliath; I will fight you." David then began the battle with Goliath.

Goliath made fun of David when he saw him, saying, "O boy, are you going to battle me with stubbornness? You will be easily crushed by my feet. Together, you are all insulting me. You sent a boy to fight a strong warrior like me.

As David prepared to fight with his faith in God, all eyes were on him. David's most important statement on the battlefield was, "God is with me, even though Goliath possesses excellent weapons. He will defend me and stand by me as I take on Goliath. With simply a sword, the battle cannot be won. With God's blessings, war is won.

David threatened Goliath, saying, "Today I will kill you, and everybody will see how God protects his loved ones."

Goliath soon started to approach David. David retrieved a stone and placed it in his sling after seeing Goliath. David rapidly swung the sling and threw the rock at Goliath.

Goliath was knocked to the ground as the stone from the sling struck him. David used Goliath's sword to sever his throat.

Israel prevailed in the conflict as the Palestinian forces fled while Goliath perished. After the battle, David praised God, saying, "Thank you, O God the Father, for taking me under your protection. Our real father is you.

Moral

Size doesn't

matter; **HEART**, **COURAGE**, **COMMITMENT,** and **Faith** that matter.

REFLECT

Why was David so confident that he could defeat Goliath?

_____
_____
_____
_____
_____
_____
_____
_____
_____
_____
_____
_____
_____
_____
_____
_____
_____
_____
_____

WHAT'S ON MY HEART

_____

_____

_____

_____

_____

_____

_____

_____

_____

MY PRAYERS

_____

_____

_____

_____

_____

_____

_____

_____

_____

_____

HADASSAH

When King Xerxes was in charge ruled the Persian Empire, he found himself looking for a wife. The kingdom's young maidens were transported to the palace for a year of beauty treatments before being presented to the king to choose his wife. Before Esther was taken, Hadassah was told not to tell anyone she was Jewish because people didn't like or trust them. So she changed her name to Esther.

The king fell in love with Esther, so he chose her as his queen. During her reign as queen, an evil man named Haman persuaded the king that all of the kingdom's Jews deserved to be slaughtered. When Mordecai learned of the plan, he immediately notified Esther, telling her that she needed to talk with the king. Esther was afraid because it was against the law to go before the king without being called. The person was only allowed into the monarch's presence if the king was delighted and held out his scepter. If he did not, they were to be killed.

Mordecai told Esther that she had to try to talk to the king, no matter what, because God had put her in a high place to save her people. Queen Esther instructed that all Jews, including herself, observe and partake in a three-day fast, after which she presented herself to the king.

The king was happy to give his wife his crown for as long as he could. She told him everything, and Haman was killed. The Jewish people were granted the right to defend themselves if anyone attacked them. Esther saved her people.

Moral

God raises people into certain positions because He plans for them and will use them to help more of His people.

REFLECT

How did the Jews survive?

WHAT'S ON MY HEART

_____

_____
_____
_____
_____
_____
_____
_____
_____

MY PRAYERS

_____

_____
_____
_____
_____
_____
_____
_____
_____

THE STORY OF JOB

Once upon a time, there lived a good man named Job. We don't know precisely when he existed, whether during Moses' time or after. His house was in the land of Uz, which was said to be on the outskirts of the desert, east of Israel. He was extremely wealthy. He owned hundreds of goats, camels, oxen, and donkeys. He was the wealthiest man in the area Job was devoted and faithful to God. Job, who lived the Lord, served God with all his heart and prayed daily at the temple altar. He was peaceful and kind, and he lived his life according to God's will. Job would go to his altar every day while his sons were working and give an offering to God. He provides an offering for each of his children and prays for them. "My children may have sinned or drifted away from God in their hearts," he said, "and I'll pray to God that they are forgiven." –

Satan replied, "from going up and down to the earth, looking at the people on it." - The LORD then said to Satan, - "I presume you've seen my loyal servant, Job? There is not another man on the earth like him. He was a good man who loved, respected, and obeyed God." - "Do you believe Job feared you for nothing?" -Then the Lord said to Satan, - "Job's sons and daughters, as well as everything he possessed, are in your hands, Satan. Do anything you want with them. However, you should not put your hands on Job, man. - Then Satan headed to earth.

Suddenly, disaster befell Job, losing everything he owned in a single day. Job was spending the day alone when one of his servants came running in. The servant then cried, - "We were feeding the cattle and donkeys when some wild men from the woods appeared and drove all of the oxen and donkeys away. And the men who were shepherding them with me were all killed. I'm the only one that made it out alive!" -While speaking, another man ran in and said, "The clouds poured rain and lightning over all the goats, and the people who looked after them were killed. I am the only one who survived."

A different man emerged before this man could even complete his sentence. He said, "Three groups of attackers who were thought to be Chaldeans came, took all the camels, and killed the men with them. I am the only one who is still alive." –

Suddenly, another man entered the room and said to Job, - "Your sons and daughters were eating and drinking together when a sudden and violent wind struck the house. I came to tell you about this because all of your sons and daughters are dead, and I am the only one that has survived." -

As a result, Job's flocks, animals, sons, and daughters were taken away from him in a single day, and his wealth vanished. Job then fell to his knees before the Lord and stated, "I came into this world with nothing, and I shall leave it with nothing.

The Lord has given and taken away; blessed be the Lord's name." - So, even when everything was taken away from him, Job did not turn away from God and held to his faith.

This was still not enough to satisfy Satan. Satan said to God, "no man will remain faithful when they are suffering themselves." God said, "do whatever you want to him, but you must spare his life". With that, Satan caused Job great suffering. Job had awful boils on him, from the sole of his feet unto the crown of his head. And Job sat in great agony; still, he did not utter one word against God.

Job would not speak against God. Then three of Job's friends came to see him and comfort him. Eliphaz, Bildad, and Zophar were their names. At that time, people believed that those suffering from illness were because God was angry with them because of their sins. People looked at Job, judged him, and said he should confess his sins. But Job stood his ground and told them that he had done nothing wrong to deserve this and still couldn't figure out why all these troubles had come to him. Yet, Job never said any hateful against God, nor said He (God) was behind his troubles.

Job did not understand the ways of Nature, but he believed that God was good; he committed himself to God's hands. At last, God spoke to Job and his friends, He told them that it was not for man to judge, and Job had done nothing wrong. Bring me an offering, and Job shall pray for you, and I will forgive you for his sake." -

So Job begged for his friends, and God forgave them. And because Job had been faithful to God, the Lord blessed Job again, healed him of the boils, and made him well. The Lord gave Job twice as much as he had previously owned. And God gave Job seven sons and three daughters again, and there were no women found so precious in all the land as Job's daughters. Because if showed such faith, Job lived under God's protection for a long time in riches, honor, and goodness.

Moral

We should not judge anyone and even God. We should not speak hate speech to God. We must always learn to respect God, remember Him in times of trouble and never blame Him just like Job did.

158

REFLECT

If God chose Job in part because of his faith, how do we use this story to encourage us toward faith?

WHAT'S ON MY HEART

_____

_____

_____

_____

_____

_____

_____

_____

_____

MY PRAYERS

_____

_____

_____

_____

_____

_____

_____

_____

_____

DANIAL

AND

THE LION DEN

King Darius was the ruler of Babylon. He had named several persons as advisors, troops, and ministers. Daniel was named as the advisors' leader. He was a devout Christian with a strong belief in Christ. Others, on the other hand, disliked Daniel and wished to have him removed from his position.

They formulated a strategy and presented it to the king. The objective was to persuade the king to pass new legislation mandating that Babylonians only pray to King Darius. Anyone who is caught praying to someone other than King Darius will be punished and thrown into the lion's den. Although Daniel knew a new law, he could not stop praying to God. Monarch Darius adored him, but when the other men objected to Daniel's prayers, the king had no choice but to punish Daniel.

'May your God rescue you, Daniel,' King Darius exclaimed as he locked Daniel in the lion's den. Daniel exhibited no signs of being concerned and began praying to Christ.

The following day, King Darius paid a visit to Daniel's den and asked if he was ok. In response to the king's anxiety, Daniel exclaimed, "My lord majesty, my God has stopped the mouths of lions and kept me safe." When King Darius heard this, he opened the door and let Daniel out. Everyone was shocked when Daniel came out of the cave alive and well. The men who plotted against Daniel were punished, and King Darius issued a law ordering the people of Babylon to fear Daniel's God.

Moral

God is mightier than any of our fears. Therefore, trusting and honoring the almighty will ensure we are on the right path.

REFLECT

What is something that scared you, but you succeeded through your faith in God?

WHAT'S ON MY HEART

_____

_____

_____

_____

_____

_____

_____

_____

_____

MY PRAYERS

_____

_____

_____

_____

_____

_____

_____

_____

_____

JONAH AND THE WHALE

Jonah was a prophet and a holy man in the land of Israel. But when God told Jonah to go to a violent city full of bad people, he was horrified. He boarded a ship and sailed away. Jonah, on the other hand, could not get away from God. God agitated the sea and caused it to become stormy. The ship had begun to sink. 'Jonah felt sorry for the sailors on board. God is angry with me. Not you, Jonah told them. Throw me into the ocean so that you can save yourself.

The sailors were at a loss for what to do. When the storm worsened, they tossed Jonah into the water to save themselves and the ship. As Jonah submerged further into the ocean, the storm disappeared. God was pleased that Jonah had thought of the sailors rather than himself. So, God ordered a whale to swallow Jonah. Inside the belly of the whale, Jonah traveled to safety. He had learned to obey God.

Moral

With faith in God, nothing is impossible.

REFLECT

_____
_____
_____
_____
_____
_____
_____
_____
_____
_____
_____
_____
_____
_____
_____
_____
_____
_____

WHAT'S ON MY HEART

MY PRAYERS

A VISIT FROM AN ANGEL

Gabriel, God's messenger angel, paid a visit to Mary, a young woman living in Nazareth. "Hello, Mary, The Lord is with you," Gabriel spoke. The appearance of the angel took Mary entirely by surprise.

Gabriel responded, "You have nothing to worry about since God loves you. I am here to tell you that You're going to have a baby, and you'll name him Jesus. He'll be a great leader.

He will be the son of God so that he will be a man. "How is that possible?" Mary wondered. Gabriel responded. "Nothing is impossible with God." Mary believed the angel. "I am, and I'm thankful to be so blessed! "She exclaimed joyfully.

Mary and her husband Joseph were soon going to have a baby. However, they needed to go to Bethlehem to pay their taxes. When they arrived in Bethlehem, they were greeted with joy. Mary's child was ready to be born.

In Bethlehem, there was no place to stay.

Because there was no room at the inn, Mary and Joseph decided to rest with the animals in a stable manger nearby; in the stable, surrounded by animals, baby Jesus was born.

Mary and Joseph were both delighted. The baby Jesus slept safe and sound in a manger, wrapped in a blanket. And God was thrilled to have a son.

Moral

Jesus is the Savior of mankind.

REFLECT

Why was it important that Jesus was born?

_____
_____
_____
_____
_____
_____
_____
_____
_____
_____
_____
_____
_____
_____
_____
_____
_____
_____
_____
_____

WHAT'S ON MY HEART

_____
_____
_____
_____
_____
_____
_____
_____
_____

MY PRAYERS

_____
_____
_____
_____
_____
_____
_____
_____

THE SHEPHERDS
AND THE
THREE WISE MEN

On the night of Jesus' birth, angels paid a visit to three shepherds tending to their flocks. "Today, God's son was born," an angel declared. He will be the King of the Jews. He is safe in Bethlehem."

Then all the angels sang, "Joy to God in the highest, and peace, good will toward men on Earth!" The shepherds went to see the newborn Jesus in the manger after the angels had left. Everyone was thrilled that they had come.

The shepherds loved baby Jesus, and they spread the word about him over the world. And Mary recognized the baby as a savior, sent by God, who would grow up to be a great man.

Three wise men noticed a bright new star in the eastern sky at this time. The star indicated that the King of the Jews had been born. They informed King Herod of Israel of the news. Herod was concerned about this. He desired to be the only King.

To find the baby King, Herod told the wise men to find baby Jesus. Herod had planned to kill him in secret. The wise men followed the star to Bethlehem, where they found Jesus. They presented him with gold and spices as gifts. God told the three wise men in a dream that night not to inform King Herod where baby Jesus was. They took an alternate route home to avoid Herod and did not notify him where Jesus was.

Moral

God makes every effort to reach every person on earth with His message, no matter how far away they are from Him.

REFLECT

God's favor comes into the world through Mary's cooperation with the angelic message she receives from God, despite her doubts/uncertainties. What doubts/uncertainties do you need to overcome to receive God's favor?

WHAT'S ON MY HEART

_____

_____
_____
_____
_____
_____
_____
_____
_____
_____
_____
_____

MY PRAYERS

_____

_____
_____
_____
_____
_____
_____
_____
_____
_____
_____

DEVIL IN THE DESERT

Jesus had been fasting in the desert for forty days and nights. He was hungry and alone. The devil approached Jesus and tried to persuade Him to convert the stones into bread, but Jesus replied that man does not live on bread alone but God's Word.

The devil then took Jesus to the highest point in the Holy City. He advised Jesus to jump from the cliff since the Bible declared the angels would save him. But Jesus responded by telling him not to put the Lord to the test.

The devil sought to entice Jesus by promising him the world's kingdom if he bent down and worshipped him. But Jesus reprimanded the devil, telling him that only God is worthy of worship. The devil then left Jesus, and the Lord's angels appeared to care for Him.

Moral

If you hold fast to the Word of God, then nobody will be able to cause you to stumble.

186

REFLECT

What is the difference between a test and a temptation? Who tests and who tempts? What is the end goal of a test compared to a temptation?

WHAT'S ON MY HEART

_____
_____
_____
_____
_____
_____
_____
_____
_____
_____

MY PRAYERS

_____
_____
_____
_____
_____
_____
_____
_____
_____
_____

JESUS CALMS THE STORM

After a long day of teaching to the people, Jesus and His disciples were aboard a boat, and Jesus fell asleep. A violent storm struck them without warning, and they were scared that they would all drown.

They awoke Jesus in fear and begged Him to save them. "Why are you so terrified, you of little faith?" Jesus asked them. Then Jesus turned to the storm and chastised it. Once again, the wind and the seas were perfectly calm. When His disciples saw His strength, they were astounded by his power.

Moral

All things can be done through faith in God

REFLECT

Can Jesus calm your fears? How do you think he does that?

WHAT'S ON MY HEART

_____
_____
_____
_____
_____
_____
_____
_____
_____

MY PRAYERS

_____
_____
_____
_____
_____
_____
_____
_____
_____
_____
_____

FAITHFUL DAUGHTER

A ruler came to Jesus and bowed before him, pleading with him to accompany him to his home to raise his daughter from the dead. Jesus had to place his hands on her shoulders and pray.

YES! Jesus agreed, and as he went to the girl's house, many people came to witness this great miracle. The group included a woman who had been bleeding for twelve years and needed help. She believed that if she could get her hands on His clothing, she would be healed. When Jesus sensed her strength slipping away, he looked to discover who was to blame. She was worried that Jesus was upset with her, but this was not the case; Jesus was delighted with her. "Take heart, daughter," he continued, "because your faith has made you well."

When Jesus arrived at the ruler's house, He took the young girl's hand in his and lifted her, alive and well.

Moral

Miracles through Jesus are possible; all you have to do is have faith.

REFLECT

What one thing can you focus on learning about God to deepen your faith in him?

WHAT'S ON MY HEART

_____

_____

_____

_____

_____

_____

_____

MY PRAYERS

_____

_____

_____

_____

_____

_____

_____

_____

_____

THE VOICE ON THE MOUNTAINTOP

Jesus led Peter, James, and John up to the highest point of the Mountain. It was there when Jesus underwent his transformation. His appearance was as radiant as the sun. His clothing started to glow. Jesus was suddenly confronted by the presence of Moses and Elijah, who then spoke with him. "Should we pitch three tents?" Peter asked. one for Moses, one for Elijah, and one for you to worship?" As Peter spoke, a dazzling mist surrounded them. A voice resounded from within the cloud and said, "This is my cherished Son." I take pleasure in his company. Hear him out! In shock, the disciples collapsed to the ground. When they looked up, there was no one else there but Jesus.

Moral

The Mountain symbolizes the spirit that guides humanity, redefines the unknown, and brings peace.

REFLECT

What was the reason for going to the highest point on the mountain?

WHAT'S ON MY HEART

_____

_____

_____

_____

_____

_____

_____

_____

_____

_____

_____

MY PRAYERS

_____

_____

_____

_____

_____

_____

_____

_____

_____

_____

THE SOWER & THE SEED

When Jesus was with his disciples and teaching all the people who came to hear him, He frequently spoke in parables. A parable is a fictional story that Jesus created to teach a lesson. Do you remember the fairytale of little red riding hood? Like a parable, these stories are easy to remember. So that people can remember them; this is often why Jesus spoke in parables.

The difference between stories and parables is that most stories are too imaginative. However, while the stories Jesus presented were not true, they were about actual events. They were intended for people and did not include cartoons or imaginary characters. After telling a parable, Jesus would explain what it meant. The farmer's parable is an example of a more extended parable.

Jesus had gone outside and was sitting by himself by the lake. Soon, many people came and gathered around Him. Then he started telling them stories. The story he told was about, A farmer who went out to prepare his garden for planting. While he was putting the seeds in the ground, some fell on the nearby walkway, where birds ate them.

The following seeds fell on rocks that the farmer had piled up nearby. Because there was little earth around the pebbles, the seeds sprouted and grew the next day. When seeds aren't placed in the ground, they don't develop roots that keep them strong and healthy, which allows them to grow correctly. Because they had no base in the ground, the little plants that had started to grow amid the rocks wilted and died because they didn't have a proper foundation.

Some seeds fell among the weeds and thorns that the farmer hadn't taken out as he continued to pour seeds onto the ground. The thorns grew quicker and taller than the seeds, preventing the seeds from getting enough sunlight and killing them.

Finally, some seeds dropped on the good soil the farmer had prepared by digging holes for the seeds. Those seeds grew into plants, which provided an abundance of food.

The disciples questioned Jesus after he told the parable. He knew they would pay attention and want to learn more about him, so he told them what it meant.

Similar to how you would listen to your Sunday School instructor, parents, or minister. They're attempting to teach you about God and how to find Him. They are planting a seed in your mind whenever they interact with you. The seed is the story about Jesus's life and how that develops and widens in-depth as you discover more information about him.

Moral

The man represents God, and the seed is His message. Just as a planted seed starts to grow, the word of God begins to deepen and grow within a person. Some seed fell on the path, and the birds ate.

REFLECT

The story Jesus tells about the sewer and the seed is a farmer planting seeds can help to think about how we listen. Jesus talks about the birds, rocks, and thorns as symbols to demonstrate thing which can keep us from growing healthy in our minds.

What's things can distract me from being a good listener to God, my parents and my teachers?

WHAT'S ON MY HEART

MY PRAYERS

JESUS WALKS ON WATER

One day, Jesus instructed his disciples to board a boat and travel across a lake to the other side. The boat carrying the apostles was rocked back and forth by the wind and seas. It grew stormy on the water. While the students went out onto the lake, Jesus went to a mountaintop to pray by himself.

Jesus realized that his friends were in danger. The only way he could get to them was to walk on water. The apostle Peter inquired, "Is that a ghost walking on water?" He was terrified. Jesus responded, "It is I, your friend, who is calling. Don't be afraid." "If it's you," Peter replied, "Then let me walk on water." Come,' Jesus said." Peter took a step closer to Jesus. However, as he noticed the waves around him, he became terrified and began to sink. Please, Lord, save me!" Peter sobbed. "Why didn't you trust in me?" Jesus questioned, stretching out his hand and pulling Peter up. The winds ceased blowing as Jesus and Peter walked across the lake toward the boat. The water began to slow down. Then everyone in the boat confessed their faith in Jesus and declared, "It is true. You, the son of God.

Moral

Focus on Jesus, and do not doubt.

REFLECT

Why is trusting in the Lord so important ?

WHAT'S ON MY HEART

_____

_____

_____

_____

_____

_____

_____

_____

_____

_____

_____

MY PRAYERS

_____

_____

_____

_____

_____

_____

_____

_____

_____

_____

_____

UPON YOU I WILL BUILD MY CHURCH

During their time in Caesarea Philippi, Jesus asked his followers, "Who do the people say that I am?" "Some people think you are John the Baptist. Others refer to Elijah. Then some believe you to be Jeremiah or a prophet. Who do you think I am? Jesus asked. Peter raised his voice. You are the Christ, the Son of the living God. Jesus answered, "Peter, you are blessed." "No person told you this. It has been revealed to you by my heavenly Father. Upon this rock, I will build my church. And the church I'm going to establish will be more powerful than the gates of hell. Peter, you are a stone in that foundation. "Don't tell anyone I'm the Christ," he cautioned them strongly. He started by explaining to his disciples what was about to take place, saying, "I'll go to Jerusalem. There, I will endure terrible pain before finally meeting my end. I'll come back from death in three days. Peter uttered those famous words, "God forbid, Lord." "You must never experience this!" Jesus scolded Peter. "If you continue to think that way, you will prevent me from achieving my goals. Your remarks come from the devil. You consider me to be a human ruler. You must realize that God sent me just for these things to unfold.

Moral

God has saved his people through Christ

REFLECT

Who did Peter say Jesus was? What was going to happen to Jesus in Jerusalem?

WHAT'S ON MY HEART

_____
_____
_____
_____
_____
_____
_____
_____
_____
_____

MY PRAYERS

_____
_____
_____
_____
_____
_____
_____
_____
_____
_____
_____

THE
LOST SHEEP

The majority of the Pharisees were opposed to Jesus because He ate with sinners and allowed them to follow Him. To help them comprehend,

Jesus told them this story. "If one of you owns 100 sheep and one of them becomes lost, will you not abandon the rest and go in search of the lost sheep?" When you find it, you are overjoyed and announce to everyone that you have found your missing sheep. You'll call your friends and have a party. Similarly, when a sinner repents, heaven has a grand celebration."

Moral

Jesus came to save those who are lost and will never give up on you.

222

REFLECT

Why would the shepherd leave the ninety-nine remaining sheep to go searching for the one that was lost?

WHAT'S ON MY HEART

_____

_____
_____
_____
_____
_____
_____
_____
_____

MY PRAYERS

_____

_____
_____
_____
_____
_____
_____
_____
_____

THE TEN VIRGINS

When Jesus told His disciples a story about ten virgins who went out to meet a bridegroom, they were amazed. Five of them were fools, while the other five were wise. The fools took their lamps but not their oil with them. The five wise women brought extra oil in jars with them. The bridegroom took a long time to arrive, and the women quickly fell asleep. All of their lamps had burned out.

At midnight, there was a shout that the bridegroom was on his way and that everyone should greet him. The five foolish women approached the wise women and asked if they might borrow some oil. The wise women refused, stating that there was not enough oil for one lamp and that they should go out and purchase more.

The bridegroom arrived on their way to buy the oil, and the wise women greeted him and invited him into the reception hall. They were refused when the other five returned and sought to be let in.

Moral

Live your lives pleasing to God because you never know when the time will come for Him to take you home.

REFLECT

What am I doing to please God?

_____
_____
_____
_____
_____
_____
_____
_____
_____
_____
_____
_____
_____
_____
_____
_____
_____
_____
_____
_____

WHAT'S ON MY HEART

_____
_____
_____
_____
_____
_____
_____
_____
_____

MY PRAYERS

_____
_____
_____
_____
_____
_____
_____
_____
_____

THE LAST SUPPER

Jesus hosted a supper for his disciples. One of the disciples, named Judas, had become a traitor. Jesus' adversaries had hired Judas to inform them where Jesus would be that night in Jerusalem. Jesus ate bread, drank wine, and shared with his disciples at the supper table.

"Take this wine and this bread, and remember me as you drink and eat it," he said. Before he died, Jesus told his disciples that one of them would hurt him. I offer him a piece of bread." Judas, the traitor, received the bread from him. Jesus answered him. "Do what needs to be done." And Judas went to Jesus.

"I must leave you for a little while," Jesus said. Believe in God, and believe in me. I'll return to comfort you." Jesus knew he would die and then return to show everyone the way to Heaven.

Moral

When we take the Lord's Supper (Communion), we must remember Jesus' sacrifice. Jesus loved us so much that He gave His body and blood for us, so we could be forgiven when we sin. That is a lot of love for every one of us.

REFLECT

What lessons did the disciples

learn at the last supper?

WHAT'S ON MY HEART

_____
_____
_____
_____
_____
_____
_____
_____

MY PRAYERS

_____
_____
_____
_____
_____
_____
_____
_____
_____
_____

THE CROSS
&
THE RESURRECTION

Judas told Jesus where he was. When the soldiers arrived. Jesus walked with them in peace. Because God had planned it from the beginning, he knew they wanted to kill him.

Jesus' enemies did not believe he was God's son. "Crucify him!" they demanded, and Jesus was nailed to the cross. "To a wooden cross, join his hands and feet. "Father, forgive them," Jesus murmured to God, "because they do not realize what they are doing." Then he passed away.

The disciples of Jesus were grieved, but they knew they would see him again soon. Joseph, a wealthy man, grabbed Jesus' body and buried it. Joseph used a large stone to block the entrance and had guards watch over the tomb.

A large earthquake struck as a woman named Mary was visiting the tomb. She saw an angel appear and roll the stone from the tomb's entrance away. The guards fainted out of panic upon seeing the angel. Mary heard the angel say to her,

"Do not be alarmed. I know you're looking for Jesus, but he's nowhere to be found. Inform his friends that he is still alive." And Mary broke the great news that Jesus had risen from the dead.

Moral

Jesus was separated from God because of our sin and its consequences. The cross also teaches us about forgiveness. Jesus is the ultimate sacrifice for sin for all time. The cross teaches us that **forgiveness takes sacrifice, even on our part toward others**.

REFLECT

Why didn't Jesus just get down
from the cross if He was God?

_____
_____
_____
_____
_____
_____
_____
_____
_____
_____
_____
_____
_____
_____
_____
_____
_____
_____
_____
_____

WHAT'S ON MY HEART

_____
_____
_____
_____
_____
_____
_____
_____
_____

MY PRAYERS

_____
_____
_____
_____
_____
_____
_____
_____
_____
_____
_____

JESUS HEALS THE PARALYZED MAN

When Jesus visited one of Capernaum's homes, a crowd gathered around Him. There was no place left, even outside the door, because so many people had come. People pushed each other to get in; others gathered outside to see or hear Jesus as He came out.

When four men learned that Jesus was coming to town, they brought their paralyzed friend to Him to see whether their friend could be healed. After arriving at the house where Jesus was staying, they knew there was no way they would be able to get through to see Him.

The man they were carrying was becoming increasingly heavy and was eager to see Jesus. They had to visit Jesus today because they didn't know how long He would be in town!

Someone took him to the roof of the building where Jesus was staying! In those days, houses were built differently. A stairway leading up to the flat roof could be found outside most homes. Many people use this room as additional living space. It was like having a deck on your house's roof. Back then, roofs weren't made of wood but rather tiles and plaster, much like plaster and Paris.

Imagine paying close attention to Jesus when you suddenly hear something from above. Everyone comes to a halt and glances up to see what's going on as the ceiling crumbles. The paralyzed man's friends have created a hole in the roof and sat him down where Jesus was.

As the man was being lowered, I'm Jesus smiled. These men had faith in Jesus' ability to heal him, or they would not have gone to such lengths.

When Jesus saw they believed, He said, "Son, your sins are forgiven." The man didn't expect this since he came to Jesus because he wanted to walk. However, because he knew what was in this man's heart, Jesus knew what he needed. Jesus understood that being disabled would be difficult, but he also understood that not being forgiven would be even more difficult.

When some of the law teachers heard Jesus forgive the man, they were outraged, saying, "How could this man forgive sins; only God can do so." "Why are you thinking these things?" Jesus asked, knowing exactly what they were thinking. This most likely surprised the men because Jesus was aware of their thoughts!

In addition, Jesus questioned them, "Which was easier: telling the paralyzed that his sins were forgiven, or telling him to "get up, grab your mat, and walk"?

This may be difficult to understand, but I believe Jesus was attempting to persuade the teachers of the law that He was the Son of Man and that God had given Him the ability to forgive sins and heal people. An average person could not have accomplished these things only by God. "I tell you, get up, grab your mat, and go home," Jesus said to the disabled man before He finished.

The man stood up, took his mat, and walked out in front of everyone. I'm just curious as to how the man responded when he was informed he could get up and go home.

Moral

It is far more critical to have our sins forgiven because our sins separate us from God, deny us eternal life, and place us under God's just judgment. By forgiving this man's sin, Jesus gives him a more extraordinary gift than physical healing.

REFLECT

What two miracles did Jesus
perform for the paralyzed man?

_____
_____
_____
_____
_____
_____
_____
_____
_____
_____
_____
_____
_____
_____
_____
_____
_____
_____
_____

WHAT'S ON MY HEART

MY PRAYERS

RUTH AND NAOMI

A lovely family lived in a place called Moab. Elimelech, his wife Naomi, and their two sons decided to move there because of the abundance of food. Elimelech soon after died, but Naomi was not alone; she had two sons. Both of her boys married but unfortunately were killed within ten years. Naomi still had Orpah and Ruth, her sons' wives, to keep her company.

Naomi spoke to her sons' wives and told them, I plan to return to my original home, and I would like it if you would do the same and return to your initial home. May God bless you as you have blessed me." Because they were such dear friends, all women cried and hugged each other.

Orpah was reluctant to leave Naomi, but Naomi assured her that she would be okay. So Orpah returned home to her family. Ruth, however, would not go no matter what Naomi said. "Please don't make me leave. I'll go where you go and remain where you stay. Your friends and family will become my friends and family, and your God will become my God."

It was fortunate that Ruth accompanied Naomi because Bethlehem was a long distance away, and Naomi would not have been able to make the trip by herself. As a result, Ruth and Naomi reunited in Bethlehem. Ruth never complains and is a wonderful friend to Naomi. She didn't expect anything in return; all she wanted to do was help.

When they arrived, Ruth decided that she needed to do some work. It was harvest season, so she went out into the fields and followed behind the harvesters, picking up any fallen barley.

Ruth was in the field when the field owner came by to meet the harvesters. He inquired about her with one of the harvesters. "All I know is that she returned from Moab with Naomi." Boaz, the property owner, was a gentleman who believed in God, which was fortunate for Ruth. He was also related to Elimelech (Naomi's deceased husband).

When Boaz went to speak with Ruth, he told her, "Stay here with the other servant girls and don't go work in the fields. I'll keep an eye on you. "Why are you being so good to me? I'm not even from here," Ruth knelt down to Boaz when she heard this. Boaz answered, "I know what you did for Naomi; you abandoned your family and relocated to a new location. May the Lord bless you for your generosity."

Ruth thanked Boaz and returned to her work in the scorching heat. Boaz even instructed his employees to drop additional barley so Ruth might have more.

Ruth took the barley home with her and shared it with Naomi. In the end, Ruth married Boaz, and everyone was happy!

Moral

Being a good friend is something that takes time. A good friend is loyal, which means you keep your promises and are a friend even when you don't feel like it. Everyone makes mistakes, and no one is perfect. You wouldn't want to be forgotten because you made a mistake.

REFLECT

> What lesson did you learn from
> Ruth and Naomi

_____

_____

_____

_____

_____

_____

_____

_____

_____

_____

_____

_____

_____

_____

_____

_____

_____

_____

WHAT'S ON MY HEART

_____

MY PRAYERS

_____

JOHN THE BAPTIST

When Elizabeth, Mary's older sister, became pregnant with John, she was pretty old. Zechariah, John's father, was told by an angel of the Lord that his son would be filled with the Holy Spirit when he was born and that he would be called John.

A lot of people thought John was crazy. He lived in the desert and preached the word of God, predicting that Jesus would come to save us. He spent a lot of time baptizing and teaching people to repent their sins. When Jesus went to John to be baptized, John was overjoyed, and Jesus was overcome by the Holy Spirit. At that moment, a voice from above said, "This is my Son, for whom I am grateful."

Moral

God is real and speaks to those who listen and believe in Him.

REFLECT

In what ways has God spoken to you?

_____
_____
_____
_____
_____
_____
_____
_____
_____
_____
_____
_____
_____
_____
_____
_____
_____
_____
_____
_____
_____
_____

WHAT'S ON MY HEART

_____

_____

_____

_____

_____

_____

_____

_____

MY PRAYERS

_____

_____

_____

_____

_____

_____

_____

_____

SERMON ON THE MOUNT

On that particular day, large groups gathered to hear Jesus speak. Jesus climbed to the top of a mountain in Galilee, sat down, and began to teach. To begin, Jesus started with the Beatitudes. The Beatitudes are a collection of sayings explaining the many blessings believers get from God.

1. Blessed *are* the poor in spirit: for theirs is the kingdom of heaven. To be poor in spirit indicates that we do not attach emotional value to our material possessions. All our earthly possessions are meaningless since we cannot carry them to heaven, which will be far more wonderful than we can imagine. God blessed you with all these beautiful things; we should be grateful for them and willing to give them up or share them with others.

2. "Blessed *are* they that mourn, for they shall be comforted." Mourning is a state of extreme sadness. You may have shed tears in the past because of physical pain or the passing of a loved one, but this is not the same thing. This involves feeling a great deal of anger toward the people around you who are unaware of God. You may not think about these things much right now, but as you get closer to God, they will become more important to you. When we need comfort, God promises to provide it.

3. "Blessed *are* the meek: for they shall inherit the earth." Being patient, not being easily upset, and not thinking too highly of oneself are all characteristics of humble people. The Pharisees were a horrible example of this in the Bible. They would make it known that they were fasting and praying and appear to be proud of what they were accomplishing for God. Except God expects us to do these things without putting on a show for others, but for God's sake and not for others' approval. It's lovely to do something nice and kind for someone, but we can always do more.

4. Blessed *are* they which hunger and thirst after righteousness: for they shall be filled. Being righteous on our own is impossible. Can we always do what is right in God's eyes? Absolutely not, and God is well aware of that. We may do our best to do the right thing; if we don't, we can ask for forgiveness and guidance.

5. "Blessed *are* the merciful: for they shall obtain mercy." Being nice and kind to others is having mercy. This includes showing love and kindness to those you may not even know.

6. "Blessed *are* the pure in heart: for they shall see God." Being pure at heart is your actions, not having any opposing thoughts or motives behind them. Like the heart that beats inside your chest. it pumps blood to keep us alive, but if something is wrong with our heart, it

doesn't work right. Jesus refers to the parts of our minds where decisions are made, the reasons for our actions, and our thoughts. God promises that we will understand Him more if we keep our minds, ideas, and decisions pure.

7. "Blessed *are* the peacemakers: for they shall be called the children of God." The simplest way to explain this is for someone who makes peace. Helping others to get along would be a big part of it. The second part of this beatitude says: then you will be called the children of God. Being God's child would mean that you are part of God's family and that you're starting to be more like Him, just like we are with our parents.

8. Blessed *are* they which are persecuted for righteousness sake: for theirs is the kingdom of heaven. God knows that being who He wants is not how the world acts. By doing the opposite of the word, we will be made fun of or worse because people don't understand why we don't do things only for ourselves. Living a life doing things for others confuses the way the world thinks. Many people around the globe want beauty and money and don't care about others as long as they get what they want. This is opposite to the life God wants us to lead. Doing the right thing isn't easy, but God wants us to know that the kingdom of heaven is waiting for us if we can get through the tough times in this life.

At the end of the Beatitudes, Jesus tells us that we ought to be joyful and delighted because if we follow his teachings, we shall be rewarded with fantastic treasures in paradise.

Following these instructions will bring us blessings from God, but it will be difficult work. All of us are still learning how to live only for God. Do not allow yourself to become disheartened. God encourages us to stand out from the crowd. Remember that it is impossible to follow the beatitudes without God's assistance. He wants to be a part of your decisions and everything you do.

Jesus didn't give these beatitudes to us with the intent of having us fail. He wanted to give us goals and something to strive for throughout our lives. He desires us to put forth our best efforts to bestow a blessed life and a greater reward in heaven someday.

Moral

You're never too young to serve Jesus!

REFLECT

What makes God's kingdom so
different from earthly kingdoms?

_____
_____
_____
_____
_____
_____
_____
_____
_____
_____
_____
_____
_____
_____
_____
_____

WHAT'S ON MY HEART

MY PRAYERS

THE

GOOD SAMARITAN

Jesus was speaking to his followers when one listener asked. "How can I achieve eternal life?" Jesus answered, "By loving God, loving yourself, and loving your neighbor." The listener asked, who is this neighbor I must follow? Jesus explained this by telling the people a story. "

One day a man was traveling from Jerusalem to Jericho, but robbers beat the man, took his clothes, and left him severely wounded and unable to get to safety. A priest walked by but refused to help the man. A Levite passed by but ignored the wounded man and went his way. Jesus now asked the people, which of the three – the priest, the Levite, and the Samaritan – do you think was a neighbor to the robbed man?"

Who do you think was a good neighbor to the hurt man?" The listener replied, "The Samaritan who helped him." Jesus told the listener, "Go and help those who need it."

Moral
Love all beings as you would love God.

REFLECT

What way can you help others?

WHAT'S ON MY HEART

_____

_____

_____

_____

_____

_____

_____

_____

MY PRAYERS

_____

_____

_____

_____

_____

_____

_____

_____

MARY AND MARTHA

Jesus was walking through a town when he came to Martha's house. Mary, Martha's younger sister, was greatly interested in what Jesus had to say. Mary sat at Jesus' feet, listening intensely as he spoke.

Martha, on the other hand, was quite busy. She washed clothes, cleaned the house, and baked bread. Martha noticed that Mary was not assisting her. Instead, she was listening to Jesus. Martha was irritated by the fact that she had to do all of the housework by herself. Martha expressed her displeasure to Jesus.

"Mary hasn't helped and left me with all the work." "Martha, you are a hard worker, but Mary is an excellent listener," Jesus replied while I was still here. Listening is essential. "Come hang out with us."

Moral Giving attention to Jesus over our problems

REFLECT

Why is it important to Jesus
that we are good listeners?

_____
_____
_____
_____
_____
_____
_____
_____
_____
_____
_____
_____
_____
_____
_____
_____
_____

WHAT'S ON MY HEART

_____
_____
_____
_____
_____
_____
_____
_____
_____
_____
_____

MY PRAYERS

_____
_____
_____
_____
_____
_____
_____
_____
_____
_____
_____

THE

PRODIGAL SON

There was once a man who was the father of two sons. The younger son was impatient to receive his share of the family money. He was eager to receive his fortune as soon as possible. As a result, his father gave him the money. The son moved to a different country. There, he had a good time and spent his money freely. He soon found himself with nothing. He became poor. He attempted to labor for food as a humble servant, but no one would hire him.

He thought, "My father's pigs eat better than I do." "It's best if I work as a servant in his home." However, he was anxious about returning to his father. He feared his father would be angry with him for leaving home and spending his money. But, because he missed his family, he decided to go anyhow. "Father, I've made a mistake," he said when he saw him. I am a sinner who is unworthy of the title of your son. Please make me a servant of yours.

On the other hand, his father was delighted to see his long-lost son and forgave him. "Says the father." "Let's have a good time!" My son had gone missing and has finally returned. He also threw a celebration to welcome his son home.

Moral, it doesn't matter how far we stray from our father. We recognize the mistake and do our best to make it right.

REFLECT

How was the prodigal son
received by his father?

WHAT'S ON MY HEART

_____

_____

_____

_____

_____

_____

_____

_____

MY PRAYERS

_____

_____

_____

_____

_____

_____

_____

_____

THE
TAX COLLECTOR

While traveling through the town of Jericho, Jesus demonstrated to the entire world what it means to hate sin rather than the sinner. Many people followed him as he made his way through the town. They wanted to hear Jesus speak about God's Kingdom!

In a crowd was a guy named Zaccheus, who worked as a tax collector. He, too, wished to see Jesus. However, he couldn't see over the crowd because he was short.

So Zaccheus had a brilliant idea. He went to the top of a tree to see Jesus better. As he passed beneath the tree, Jesus looked up and said, "Zaccheus, come down; I have to stay with you today." Zaccheus, overjoyed, stepped down and began walking with Jesus back to his house.

On the other hand, the crowd was not delighted with the change of plans. Most people in Jericho despised tax collectors because they were selfish and dishonest.

The disciples of Jesus did not want their savior to show mercy to such a sinner. But Zaccheus had changed. As a pledge to Jesus, he stated that he would give half of his earnings to the poor and repay the money he had taken.

This is exactly what Jesus wished for. He blessed Zaccheus and proved that it is better to hate the sin than the sinner.

Moral

Hate the sin, not the sinner.

288

REFLECT

Write a letter of forgiveness to someone who has wronged you.

WHAT'S ON MY HEART

_____

_____
_____
_____
_____
_____
_____
_____
_____
_____

MY PRAYERS

_____

_____
_____
_____
_____
_____
_____
_____
_____
_____
_____
_____

THE ASCENSION

After rising from the grave, Jesus spent 40 days with his disciples. He taught many things to his devoted disciples and assured them that he would return in the future. "You shall be baptized with the Holy Spirit soon," he stated. Then you will receive the power of God. You will inform the people of Jerusalem and the rest of the world about my story." Jesus prayed for his disciples and gave them his blessing. Then, Jesus was covered in bright light as they looked at him. He was taken to the heavens and then vanished. After that, John, a devout disciple of Jesus, prayed and saw heaven. It was a beautiful and peaceful place. John knew one day Jesus would someday return to bring his people into the Heavens.

Moral Those who believe in the Lord are never alone because the Holy Spirit lives inside their heart.

REFLECT

What significance does the event of the
Ascension of Jesus Christ have for the
Christian?

_____

_____

_____

_____

_____

_____

_____

_____

_____

_____

_____

_____

_____

_____

_____

_____

_____

_____

_____

WHAT'S ON MY HEART

_____

_____
_____
_____
_____
_____
_____
_____
_____

MY PRAYERS

_____

_____
_____
_____
_____
_____
_____
_____
_____
_____

WATER INTO WINE

When Jesus began teaching people about God and Heaven, he chose some men to accompany him on his journey. They were known as the disciples. You probably won't recall all of their names, but some of the most well-known are Simon, his brother Andrew, and James and John, who were also brothers. As they traveled together, Jesus performed many incredible miracles. The miracles Jesus performed no one else has been able to do. Don't we know how he did them? God was with him.

Jesus and his disciples were invited to attend a wedding in Cana. Everyone seemed to have a good time, eating, drinking, and dancing. Someone suddenly announced, "There is no more wine."

Everyone came to a halt and grumbled. Mary, Jesus' mother, was present and addressed her son, saying, "Can't you do something?" For a brief period, Jesus pondered.
He instructed, "Bring those water pots over here and ensure they are full."

The servants followed his instructions and filled the pots with water before placing them in front of Jesus. "Now," Jesus said. "Take a cup of water and give it to the master to taste."

He took a sip. He said, "It's wine!" "Wonderful wine!" It's far better than the wine we drank at the beginning of the wedding!" The disciples smiled as they turned to face Jesus. They said, "Changing water into wine is a true miracle."

Moral

Jesus can provide for our needs. We may not get everything we want, but the power of the Lord can meet your needs to empower you to pursue a deeper relationship with God.

REFLECT

What is the difference between water
and wine?

_____
_____
_____
_____
_____
_____
_____
_____
_____
_____
_____
_____
_____
_____
_____
_____
_____
_____

WHAT'S ON MY HEART

_____

_____
_____
_____
_____
_____
_____
_____
_____
_____

MY PRAYERS

_____

_____
_____
_____
_____
_____
_____
_____
_____
_____
_____

THE WOMAN AT JACOB'S WELL

Jesus and his disciples were traveling through the land of Samaria. There was a well there where the people of Sychar drew their drinking water. Jacob, the father of the Israelites, had dug the well long ago. The early afternoon was probably sunny and hot. Wearily Jesus sat down by the well while the disciples went into Sychar to buy food.

Jesus was all alone, but not for long. A woman who lived in Sychar came to draw drinking water. "Give me a drink," Jesus said to her. The woman was surprised. "How is it that you, being a Jew, ask for a drink from me, a Samaritan woman?" in those days, Jew had no dealings with Samaritans! She was probably even more surprised when Jesus said, "If you knew Who I am, you would ask me for living water." The woman said to Jesus," Sir, you have nothing to draw with, and the well is deep.

Where, then, do you get that living water? Are you greater than our father, Jacob, who gave us the well?" "Whoever drinks this water will thirst again," Jesus told the woman. "But whoever drinks the water I shall give him will never thirst. The water that I shall give will become in him a fountain of springing up into everlasting life," "Sir, give me this water."

Moral

Share the word of God. The woman at the well exemplifies love, truth, redemption, and acceptance.

REFLECT

The woman comes to believe in Jesus after a very short conversation. What would Jesus need to say to you (or what secrets would he need to know about you) to make you believe him?

WHAT'S ON MY HEART

_____
_____
_____
_____
_____
_____
_____
_____
_____

MY PRAYERS

_____
_____
_____
_____
_____
_____
_____
_____
_____
_____
_____

THE BREAD AND THE FISHES

Jesus had already prepared his twelve disciples for their mission by sending them out into the world while also giving them the ability to cure those sick and share the word of God's love. When the disciples returned to Jesus, they reported everything that had happened during their travels, including the people they had healed and spoken to. They were all quite excited to tell Jesus about their travels and the things they had experienced.

The problem was that people followed the disciples in the hope that they would lead them to Jesus. They had witnessed His miracles and desired to see more. Jesus was aware that the disciples wished to speak with Him. They hadn't even had a chance to eat when Jesus told them to "come with me," and they would find a peaceful place to talk and rest. So, they took a boat and went to a quiet place where they could speak. However, many people watched them leave, recognized them, and followed them. The wind slowed down the boat that Jesus and his disciples were traveling in, and as a result, the people arrived on the other side of the shore before Jesus, and his disciples did.

The disciples and Jesus were surprised to see such a big crowd waiting for them when they arrived. Jesus was moved by love for these people because He recognized their need for guidance and someone to teach them. Jesus knew his disciples would understand, so he started teaching the people.

It was getting late, and no one had eaten dinner yet. The disciples approached Jesus and said, "It's already late, and there isn't any food. Perhaps it would be best if we sent the people away so that they could travel to the nearby cities in search of food. Jesus, however, answered, "give them something to eat." The disciples didn't believe they had correctly heard Jesus, so they responded, "We can't feed all these people; we would have to work for practically an entire year to pay for all the food!"

One of the disciples, Andrew, was talking to Jesus when he saw a little boy walking by with some food. He asked what he had. When he saw the disciples talking to Jesus, he quickly ran over and said, "Here is a boy with five loaves of bread and two little fish, but how far will they go among so many people?"

Jesus smiled at the crowd and instructed the disciples to tell everyone to take a seat.

All five thousand of everyone took a seat on the grass. Jesus took the loaves of bread and thanked God for them after everyone had taken their seats. He proceeded in the same process with the fish. Afterward, the disciples distributed the bread among themselves, allowing each person to take as much as they desired.

Keep in mind that there were only five loaves of bread and two tiny fish, just enough for the boy to eat. Five thousand people were eating from this boy's lunch and had unlimited access to it.

Jesus instructed the disciples to collect all the food left after everyone had finished eating so that nothing would go to waste. They counted the food baskets once they had collected them. Twelve baskets from the young boy's lunch were still filled with bread and fish.

It's a miracle that his little meal even filled one of the baskets before Jesus touched it, considering how little food there was. Beyond that, he was so much more. As soon as the people recognized what had occurred, they turned to each other and said, "Jesus must be an important person sent from God."

Moral teaches us the importance of sharing, making the most of what we have, and that we must place our trust in God.

REFLECT

What is so impressive about
feeding that many people?

_____
_____
_____
_____
_____
_____
_____
_____
_____
_____
_____
_____
_____
_____
_____
_____
_____
_____
_____

WHAT'S ON MY HEART

_____

_____
_____
_____
_____
_____
_____
_____
_____

MY PRAYERS

_____

_____
_____
_____
_____
_____
_____
_____
_____
_____
_____
_____

THE STORY OF THE BLIND MAN

Jesus performed many miracles, many of which we have all heard about and witnessed. There was a moment when Jesus' disciples struggled to understand his blessings. As a result, the disciples once brought a blind man to Jesus while they were at Bethsaida.

They asked Jesus to heal the man so he could see God's unique creation. As a result, Jesus led the man out of town. After that, he spat in his eyes and rubbed them with his fingers. And then a miracle happened. The blind man who was suddenly able to see!

Moral

Trust in God, and you'll see the true beauty of his creation.

REFLECT

What Miracles have you

witnessed ?

WHAT'S ON MY HEART

_____
_____
_____
_____
_____
_____
_____
_____

MY PRAYERS

_____
_____
_____
_____
_____
_____
_____
_____
_____

THE STORY OF LAZARUS

Mary and Martha were two of Jesus' closest friends. One day, Jesus received word that one of his friends' brothers, Lazarus, was dying. Jesus was saddened at the news because he knew how much his friends loved their brother. However, he did not rush to meet the dying man since he knew God had other plans for him.

After a short time, Lazarus died. Four days after Lazarus' death, Jesus went to see his friends. But, before he could go to their house, Jesus ran into Martha. She was angry because she believed Jesus had failed them. She believed that her brother might have been rescued if Jesus had arrived sooner. "I am the resurrection and the life," Jesus told her. Anyone who believes in me will live even if they are dead."

As a result, Jesus invited Martha to accompany him to Lazarus' tomb. "Lazarus, come forth," he said as he arrived. And with those three simple words, Jesus was able to restore life to Lazarus' body!

Moral

God has a plan for our lives.

REFLECT

What is something you didn't understand at the time but worked out better?

_____
_____
_____
_____
_____
_____
_____
_____
_____
_____
_____
_____
_____
_____
_____
_____
_____

WHAT'S ON MY HEART

MY PRAYERS

THE
HEAVEN AND THE EARTH

Have you ever wondered who wrote the Bible? Do you ever wonder how they were able to decipher God's words? This is a narrative concerning a revelation that the apostle John had.

John was the blessed one who had the revelation of truth. "I was present on the day the Savior was nailed to the cross," he says. I witnessed his sorrow and pain as he died. But he was soon born again! After all, he was the Living One!

The angels then showed me even more amazing things. I saw the lovely Jerusalem and the Holy City waiting for all Christians.

I also saw the new Heaven and Earth, eagerly awaiting God's children's arrival. 'I am the Alpha and the Omega,' God said. I am everything. Nobody will ever go thirsty if they trust in me. I will feed those who are hungry. All of this was built for my children – for you. This lovely new universe is now entirely yours!'

Moral

The Bible is God's word.

REFLECT

What does Gods word mean to
you?

_____
_____
_____
_____
_____
_____
_____
_____
_____
_____
_____
_____
_____
_____
_____
_____
_____
_____
_____
_____
_____

WHAT'S ON MY HEART

_____

_____
_____
_____
_____
_____
_____
_____
_____
_____

MY PRAYERS

_____

_____
_____
_____
_____
_____
_____
_____
_____
_____

Check out my other books

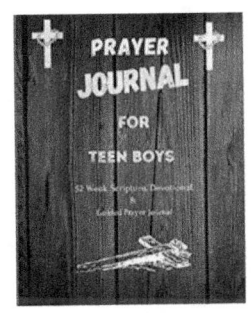

www.ingramcontent.com/pod-product-compliance
Lightning Source LLC
Chambersburg PA
CBHW081324120626

46546CB00011B/3205